Meditations
for
Mondays

52 PERSONAL

DEVOTIONS

Meditations *for* *Mondays*

TO HELP SENIOR

ADULTS START FRESH

EACH WEEK

GWEN LAM

BROADMAN
&HOLMAN
PUBLISHERS

Nashville, Tennessee

Printed in the United States of America

4253-91
0-8054-5391-1

Published by
Broadman & Holman Publishers
Nashville, Tennessee

Design: Steven Boyd

Dewey Decimal Classification: 242.65
Subject Heading: DEVOTIONAL LITERATURE \ ELDERLY
Library of Congress Card Catalog Number: 95-23222

Library of Congress Cataloging-in-Publication Data
Lam, Gwen
    Meditations for mondays: 52 personal devotions to help senior adults
start fresh each week / Gwen Lam
        p.   cm.
    Includes bibliographical references (p.   ).
    ISBN 0-8054-5391-1   (pbk)
    1. Aged—Prayer-books and devotions—English.   2. Devotional
calandars.   3. Spiritual life—Christianity.   I. Title.
BV4579.5.L36   1996
242'.2—dc20

    95-23222
    CIP

00 99 98 97 96 5 4 3 2 1

Dedicated with love
to Martin and Virginia Thomas,
who suggested that I write
these meditations,
and to the residents of
Denton Good Samaritan Village,
who read them first
and provided encouragement
and inspiration.

Preface

—

As I reviewed each meditation in this book before mailing the manuscript to the publisher, a new realization of the goodness of God overwhelmed me. I saw how He brought into my life scores of godly women and men—and young people too—who nourished my spiritual growth through the years.

Many of these meditations reflect the Christian family into which my nine brothers and sisters and I were born. Church was a central focus, though Christian education also went on at home. I recall my mother holding us spellbound as she read about David and Goliath and other tales from Hurlbut's *Story of the Bible*, always planting Christian precepts into young minds. The early training remained with us as we grew up and pursued varied vocations. Long after our parents were gone, family members continued to influence my spiritual life.

—

Most especially, I am grateful for answered prayers as I sought a deeper faith during middle age while living in New York City. The Lord taught me through Dr. Bryant Kirkland and others at Fifth Avenue Presbyterian Church; Lois Ewald, a gifted Bible teacher at Hephzibah House; and the Tuesday Twelve, a home Bible study and prayer group. I am mindful of countless Christian authors and outstanding seminar and retreat leaders.

Since retirement to Denton, Texas, my continued quest to grow has been aided at First Presbyterian Church and by participation in Bible Study Fellowship, a unique program from which I have profited enormously. The associations and rich friendships at Good Samaritan Village have fed into these meditations.

I am particularly in debt to the many family members and special friends who graciously permitted me to share their faith stories and to others who suggested topics they thought I should write about.

The quiet time experiences of a number of friends—who joined me for a brainstorming session—enriched the Personal Application sections of these devotionals. I not only incorporated many of their ideas in the book but in my own spiritual life as well. Therefore I am doubly beholden to Nan Anderson, Deanna Campbell, Yvonne Cole, Martha Cowles, Mary Evelyn Huey, Elizabeth Lomax, and Virginia Thomas.

Finally, I express deep gratitude to these four: my sister Norma, whose wise counsel and encouragement proved invaluable; Cathy Taylor, who cheerfully and patiently helped me with elementary computer perplexities; Nancy Sanders, whose editing skills increased the readability of this book; and Vicki Crumpton, editor at Broadman & Holman, whose wisdom and wit bathed this project in pure joy.

✧

Meditations for Mondays

—

My prayer is that God will help you use these meditations to give a spiritual boost to your week, drawing you into deeper fellowship with Him—that He will give you a personal message to apply to your life in the days ahead. I hope you will start a companion "Personal Application Notebook." Write down, ponder, and pray about the goal for the week. Then indicate what activities you will undertake—from the suggestions given or from other ideas prompted by the Holy Spirit. Jot down your experiences. Make Scripture verses your own by copying them into your notebook. If you don't own a hymnal, buy one and borrow the familiar words of revered songs to enhance your prayers. A few books have been recommended; your Christian bookseller can suggest others on topics of special interest.

✧

———

1. Wake-up Call

Read Isaiah 50:4–10

He awakens Me morning by morning,
He awakens My ear to hear as the learned.
Isaiah 50:4

Many retired people say they appreciate the opportunity to "sleep in" after years of getting up early to take care of family and job requirements. Others say their internal alarm clocks are set, and they continue to arise early even though nothing compels them to do so. I belong to the latter group.

"You get up at six o'clock!" exclaimed a friend. "What do you *do* with all that time?"

"Three things," I said. "I read the Bible, I pray, and I write in my journal." An incident that occurred many years ago prompted my pre-breakfast meeting with God. My older brother Elie—much to my dismay—enrolled me (a busy career woman!) in a Bible memory program. I reluctantly began the weekly memorization, feeling that if he loved me that much I should follow through.

In a few months, one verse began to haunt me, bubbling into my consciousness when I was working at my desk, sitting on a bus, or attending a business meeting. "The LORD GOD has given Me the tongue of the learned, that I should know how to speak a word in season to him who is weary. He awakens Me morning by morning, He awakens My ear to hear as the learned" (Isa. 50:4).

One night when I lay propped up in bed reading, the verse interrupted again. I closed the book, sat up and said, "Lord, if You're telling me You want me to get up earlier so You can teach me, wake me whenever You wish." With no alarm set, I woke up exactly one hour earlier than usual. This pattern continued through the next days and weeks and became firmly fixed.

When I asked God to direct the use of this extra hour, my devotional time flourished. Bible reading became more personal as I asked the Holy Spirit to help me understand it and apply it to my life. My prayers became more conversational and more focused, springing from the Bible and moving to different areas of my life. For instance, reading Numbers 14, I saw God's anger toward the Israelites for their persistent "murmurings." I asked the Lord to help me stop being a complainer.

Looking back, I see how my life began changing as I committed each day to the Lord—thanking Him, bringing Him my joys and concerns, and seeking His direction for the day ahead. Supernatural wisdom bathed my decision-making. The trials and troubles didn't cease, but they quit causing anxiety. Eventually I experienced what the apostle Paul described as peace beyond human understanding. A fresh filling of the Holy Spirit, morning by morning, continues to be my power source.

✧

My Prayer

Father, thank You for filling my life afresh each morning with Your Holy Spirit to teach and guide me. Amen.

My Goal

To know God better and grow closer to Him through daily quiet time.

My Commitment This Week

Choose two or more activities:

___ Thank God that I can meet Him one-to-one during quiet time each day to know Him better.

___ Start a "Personal Application Notebook," writing down my goal for the week and what actions I will take.

___ Preface Bible reading with a prayer that God will help me understand it and apply it to my life.

___ Pray each morning about coming daily activities.

___ Pray the words of "Just a Closer Walk with Thee."

2. Encouragers

Read Acts 9:26–31

Then Barnabas came to his help and took him to the apostles.
He explained to them how Saul had seen the Lord.
Acts 9:27, TEV

The Bible says the name *Barnabas* means "Son of Encouragement." The life of Barnabas confirmed that definition.

Barnabas helped many people, including the apostle Paul. The other apostles distrusted Paul because of his past persecution of Christians—they were skeptical of his conversion. But Barnabas boldly defended Paul, confirming the reality of Christ's call. Paul's subsequent acceptance by the apostles cleared the way for the launching of his great ministry to the Gentiles.

Most of us can recall one or more encouragers in our own lives—perhaps a parent, a teacher, or someone else who offered a reassuring word or helpful advice at a turning point.

George Washington Carver, the son of a slave woman, found Etta Budd, his art teacher, to be a major encourager in his life. She urged him to pursue scientific agriculture, guiding him to Iowa State College, where her father headed the Department of Horticulture. Carver became the school's first black student. His research led to hundreds of new products, including more than 300 from the peanut and 118 from the sweet potato.

A devout Christian, Carver said visions from God prompted his discoveries and therefore they belonged to everyone. He himself became an encourager to thousands, including fellow researchers, students, and others.

Being an encourager lies at the very heart of Christianity. Paul commended early church members for their helpfulness. He urged them to continue to "encourage one another, and help one another, just as you are now doing" (1 Thess. 5:11, TEV). How do we follow through with Paul's admonition today?

A whole cadre of retirees enjoy a satisfying second career by sharing knowledge and experience with young people just getting started. Some become foster grandparents. Others sign on as tutors, visit hospital patients, help out in nursing homes, volunteer in prison ministries, or give time at schools, youth centers, and other agencies that serve the community.

Many of us respond to less demanding situations close to home—a note, call, or visit to a shut-in; a commendation for a job well done; recognition for a thoughtful deed observed. Some older adults become "pen pals" with elementary school students. If we ask God to give us opportunities plus a willing heart, He will use us to encourage others.

✧

My Prayer

Father, thank You for all who have helped me through the years. Help me see and take advantage of opportunities to encourage others. Amen.

My Goal

To become a more effective encourager.

My Commitment This Week

Choose two or more activities:

___ Think about people who have been encouragers to me through the years and thank God for them

___ Ask the Lord to awaken me to opportunities to encourage others and help me to respond appropriately.

___ Acknowledge someone I observe doing a job well, something usually taken for granted, such as a person bagging groceries.

___ Comment personally or through a note when I hear or read something especially helpful or enjoyable.

___ Look for a good trait in one or more people each day and praise them for it (especially a young person).

3. The Memory Mystique

Read Psalm 25:6–11

Do not remember the sins of my youth, nor my transgressions; according to Your mercy remember me.
Psalm 25:7

When a high school classmate and I met for the first time in more than fifty years, we quickly began discussing our youthful experiences on the debating team. "I even remember the topic when we went to the district meet in 1938," he said.

"So do I!" I exclaimed. We immediately recited it in unison, "Resolved: That Texas Should Have a Unicameral Legislature."

Yet shortly afterward I sat in the parking lot at the supermarket trying to recall the reason why I'd come.

Finally it dawned on me that I'd meant to go to the pharmacy for medicine.

Many of us in the "three score and more" age group experience such puzzling incidents—when distant memories emerge sharp while recent ones sometimes fade. We're also realizing that some memories beg for dismissal while others bring great joy when recalled. In the delightful 1993 British movie *Enchanted April*, one of four older women going off on holiday says she wants to "sit in the shade and remember better times."

In Psalm 25, David cried out to God to *forget* the sins of his youth but to *remember* him and grant His pardon, protection, and guidance. What a sensible model prayer for us. Further, unlike David, we can rely on the assurance given in the new covenant described in Jeremiah 31:31–34. God's promise: "I will forgive their iniquity, and their sin I will remember no more" (v. 34).

Christ's promise to forgive and forget serves as a challenging reminder to us. Jesus told His disciples that if they failed to forgive others, their heavenly Father would not forgive them. When somebody hurts me, I frequently find it much easier to express forgiveness than to "remember no more." Yet my forgiveness is swallowed up in sinful self-righteousness when I lock away in a corner of my mind the wrong I've only verbally forgiven.

Celebrating Holy Communion presents a good time to exercise periodic "memory cleansing." Christ told the apostles to "do this in remembrance of Me" (Luke 22:19), as He presided over the Passover meal on the night of His betrayal. Meditating on the incomprehensible thing He did for us helps to put in perspective our sins and any resentments to which we may cling. The awesome truth—we are invited to leave them all at the Lord's table and start afresh.

✧

My Prayer

Father, this week please help me follow Your example in re-membering and forgetting. Amen.

My Goal

To remove lingering negative memories involving my actions or those about people I have not fully forgiven.

My Commitment This Week

Choose two or more activities:

____ Acknowledge unconfessed sins and thank God for forgiveness.

____ Ask God for the ability to forgive and to pray for those who wrong me or someone I love.

____ Write down on a slip of paper the initials of anyone against whom I hold a grudge and ask God to enable me to forgive and forget. Tear up the paper and discard it.

____ Write to children, grandchildren, or other younger relatives about memories of God's goodness.

____ Read 1 Corinthians 11:17–29, asking God to help me grasp the deep meaning of Communion.

4. Alive Today

Read Matthew 6:25–34

Therefore do not worry about tomorrow, for tomorrow will worry about its own things.
Matthew 6:34

Reverend Frank Wilcox, former Spiritual Ministries director of the Good Samaritan Society, spoke of a truth that came to him as he faced his terminal illness. "Not a single person has a lease on tomorrow," he said. Even as he recognized that he had fewer days ahead than he once thought there might be, he found it helpful to view life in its three-day perspective.

Yesterday . . .

. . . with all its aches and pains, mistakes, and missed opportunities, has been handed back to God. God has accepted it and has buried its inadequate performances and sins in a bottomless ocean. We need not waste a second thought in regret or remorse. Unhappy memories should be banished. Forget the negatives of yesterday.

Tomorrow . . .

. . . with all its possible adversities, burdens, suffering, and failures, also belongs to God. In His Sermon on the Mount, Jesus told His disciples not to worry about tomorrow, their life, or basic necessities. He told them that the heavenly Father knew their needs. Therefore, they should set their hearts on Him and His kingdom.

In a sense, worry can become sinful. It doubts God's faithfulness and power. Worry about tomorrow is not only futile, but medical science has found that it can actually cause a worsening of physical ailments. I thought of this connection when I asked about the nature of a woman's health problem. "Oh, most of what's wrong with her is stress-related," I was told.

Today . . .

. . . with its promise of the Lord's presence, provides a fresh opportunity for us to open ourselves to Him. We can confidently seek His guidance in the morning about the best use of the hours given to us. As we are quiet before Him, we may ask for His healing touch or His help in handling pain. Or perhaps we need His wisdom in making a decision or solving a problem.

No concern is too large or too small to lay before Him. Maybe He'll lead us to reach out to others through a visit—in person, by phone, or by letter. Perhaps we'll simply continue an activity or begin a new one. Each day, we are invited to join the psalmist in proclaiming, "This is the day which the LORD has made; we will rejoice and be glad in it" (Ps. 118:24).

✧

My Prayer

*Father, increase my ability to release worries
into Your loving hands, with a thankful heart.
Help me live each new day to the fullest
in the way most pleasing to You. Amen.*

My Goal

To focus my mind and energies on each new day, forgetting the negatives of yesterday and leaving the unknowns of tomorrow in God's hands.

My Commitment This Week

Choose two or more activities:

___ Memorize Psalm 118:24 and recite it each morning.

___ Each day, ask God to help me use the hours in a way pleasing to him.

___ Commit any nagging worries about the future to God, asking Him to show me specific actions I should take, if any.

___ Thank God for forgiving past sins, and ask Him to remove any negative thoughts that linger.

___ Read Psalm 121. Write down my responsibility and what God will do. Read it when visiting a shut-in.

✧

5. To Tell the Truth . . .

Read Proverbs 12:17–22

Lying lips are an abomination to the Lord,
but those who deal truthfully are His delight.
Proverbs 12:22

My friend was out of his car before the nearby patrolman reached the scene of the accident on a busy street in Denton, Texas.

Fortunately, neither driver was injured, though both cars were damaged. The patrolman wrote a ticket for the young woman judged to be at fault. In filling out his report, he asked if the drivers were wearing seat belts. My friend said he was.

Later, as he was talking with his insurance agent and getting estimates for the repair of his car, a troubling thought kept nagging him. Back home his discomfort continued. He got back in his car and went in search of the patrolman.

"I'm eighty-one. That's too old to start lying," he told the officer. "I'm 95 percent certain I wasn't wearing my seat belt." The officer thanked him and changed the record.

When my friend related the incident, I tried to congratulate him on his honesty. After all, only he (and God) knew the truth and it had no bearing on the accident. But he quickly brushed aside my attempt to commend him.

"I shouldn't have done it," he said. "But I'll tell you this, I *sure* felt a lot better after I corrected it."

This simple story illuminates an essential element of Christian character—a conscience alive and responsive to the nudging of the small "inner voice." I once read that when we get in the habit of shading the truth or dismissing the "little white lie" as of no consequence, our conscience can gradually get so callused that it doesn't feel the warning prick from the Holy Spirit. Then we're primed to be less than honest, telling ourselves that the falsehood does no harm. Sometimes we even experience momentary pleasure when it puts us in a better light.

Wanting to "look good" in front of the apostles and fellow church members prompted a married couple to lie—with devastating consequences (Acts 5). Ananias, after pledging the total proceeds from the sale of a parcel of land, sold it and laid the money at the apostles' feet. In reality, he had held part of the money back. When Peter confronted him with his "lie to God," Ananias dropped dead! His wife also lied, when questioned later, saying the amount contributed represented the selling price. She immediately followed her husband in death.

✧

My Prayer

*Father, keep me honest in small and large matters!
And help me be obedient to the Holy Spirit's
guidance. Amen.*

My Goal

To be truthful at all times and remain responsive to the Holy Spirit's nudging if I'm about to stray.

My Commitment This Week

Choose two or more activities:

___ Memorize Proverbs 12:22. Thank God for the indwelling Holy Spirit, who wants to help keep me honest.

___ Pray that God will guide me in remaining totally honest in all areas of my life.

___ Ask God to keep me alert to opportunities to help a young person understand the importance of honesty.

___ Ask God to show me how to respond if Christian acquaintances speak of a dishonest act they have committed.

___ Read about Ananias and his wife, who shaded the truth and suffered terrible consequences (Acts 5:1–11).

6. *Never Alone*

Read Deuteronomy 31:1–8

Be strong and of good courage . . . He is the One who goes with you. He will not leave you nor forsake you.
Deuteronomy 31:6

My mother's admonition to my oldest brother—when he was leaving for college—flashed into his mind when he faced a crisis.

Conrad had traveled from Texas to Louisiana to participate in an intercollegiate debating tournament. He sat backstage in the auditorium struggling with a sudden attack of asthma. His team had reached the finals, but he could scarcely breathe, let alone speak.

Due at the podium in less than ten minutes, Conrad moved the curtain and looked out at the audience. That's when his mother's words came to him: "Remember, you are never alone. God is always with you. Just call on Him."

Conrad closed his eyes and prayed. Almost immediately he sensed the tightness in his chest subsiding, and he gradually began to breathe normally. His team won the tournament.

The asthma attack story impressed me as a child even though I didn't fully understand it. But several years later a sequel to it taught me a lesson about my mother's faith that has reinforced my own through the years.

My brother had enrolled in medical school, and during visits home he enthralled us with his experiences. On one occasion, he said, "Mama, you know that asthma attack? I was telling one of my professors about it and he said it wasn't divine intervention. He said when I looked out at the audience, fear caused my body to produce adrenaline and that did it."

I can still see the twinkle in Mother's eye as she answered something like this: "And did he also explain who created that intricate system of organs in your body that served you so well? Did he say what force produced the fear? What prompted you to look out at the audience?"

My mother's message to her family about God's presence and dependability reminds me of Moses' message to Joshua when preparing him to lead Israel into the Promised Land. Moses spoke confidently, from firsthand knowledge. During forty years of desert wanderings, when the Israelites grumbled and rebelled and even Moses' brother and sister failed him, God remained faithful.

Many older adults count sixty, seventy, or more years of earthly wanderings with God by their side. When we became Christians, we were given a bonus, the indwelling Spirit, that not even Moses received. The Spirit stays with us to guide and strengthen. Looking back at my own life's ups and downs supports my mother's admonition and removes fear of being alone in my remaining years.

✧

My Prayer

Father, thank You for the assurance that You will always be with me. Amen.

My Goal

To remember I am never alone and to thank God and rely on Him during difficult days and good ones.

My Commitment This Week

Choose two or more activities:

___ Thank God each morning on waking up for a sense of His presence to guide me during the day.

___ Ask God to help me live so that others see my trust in Him.

___ Pray for relatives or friends experiencing health problems or other crises and tell them I am doing so.

___ Memorize Psalm 56:3. Recite to one who is fearful.

___ Read the words or sing "Blessed Assurance, Jesus Is Mine," confirming to God my reliance on Him.

7. Think Small

Read Luke 21:1–4

*And He saw also a certain poor widow
putting in two mites.*
Luke 21:2

In a bygone era when big automobiles were the rage, an award-winning advertising campaign burst on the scene, changing the focus of many car buyers. Stark, full-page advertisements featured a tiny photograph of a plain, fuel-efficient foreign car with the caption, "Think small."

The Bible reminds us of the value God placed on smallness in many areas of life. For example, Jesus proclaimed that the poor widow's offering of two copper coins surpassed that of the rich people. They gave out of their surplus; she gave her all.

Through the parable of the talents, Jesus taught the urgency of good stewardship and accountability even if given only one talent. He promised the disciples that if they just had faith the size of a mustard seed they could move mountains. Do Christians too often fail to "think small," and thereby miss moments of pleasure or peace of mind? Three reminders:

Look for, savor, and thank God for the multitude of small blessings showered on us daily. For example, a good night's rest, medicine that relieves a health problem, an "inner voice" reminding us of something urgent, a telephone, a Bible, a friend to talk to, a church to attend, convenient and well-stocked stores to shop in, a good television program to enjoy, or simply a clear, bright morning.

Combine gratitude to God with small acts of kindness to others, asking Him to open eyes, hearts, and hands to opportunities. Get ideas by looking around at the thoughtfulness of others. Consider a shut-in who would be cheered by a phone call or visit. Take along a loaf of banana bread, or plate lunches for the two of you. Give someone a ride. Offer to read to someone whose vision is diminishing. Pray about responding to one of the many needs for volunteers in your community.

Remember to talk with God about small problems that disturb our peace of mind. This point was impressed on me by the writings of Amy Carmichael, missionary to South India. "It is the minute unimportant-looking things, that are most likely to shatter our peace," she said, "because they are so small that we are very likely to fight them ourselves instead of looking up to our strong God." Nothing is too small to take to Him.

Small cars now claim a loyal following among a segment of the population. Similarly, our lives are enriched when we "see" and give thanks for small blessings, perform small services happily and well, and immediately pray about small problems.

✧

My Prayer

Father, thank You for daily blessings, for help with small problems, and for prompting me to perform small kindnesses for others. Amen.

My Goal

To remember that God places value on seemingly small areas of daily life and to respond accordingly.

My Commitment This Week

Choose two or more activities:

___ Write down and give thanks for small blessings I have too often taken for granted.

___ Extend a small act of kindness to one person daily.

___ Pray about seemingly unimportant problems that disturb my peace of mind.

___ Ask God to direct the use of talents He has given me.

___ Read and share *First We Have Coffee* by Margaret Jensen.

8. Doubt: Harmful or Helpful?

Read Matthew 11:1–10

Are You the Coming One, or do we look for another?
Matthew 11:3

Even John the Baptist, God's prophet who introduced Christ to Israel, experienced doubts. At one point he specifically wondered whether Jesus was really the promised Messiah. At the time, John was languishing in a dark dungeon, so his uncertainty was understandable. Also, Christ had turned out to be a far different person from the kingly monarch expected.

John didn't dwell on his doubts or give up in disbelief and despair. Instead, he dispatched two of his disciples to quiz Jesus. Jesus told the emissaries to report to their leader what He was doing: healing the lepers, the deaf, the blind, and the lame, and preaching the gospel to the poor. In fact, Jesus was fulfilling the prophecy of Isaiah, the very book John had been quoting from.

Another man close to Jesus who boldly expressed his doubts was Thomas. When his fellow disciples told him they had actually seen Jesus after His resurrection, Thomas said that he would have to see the nail prints in His hands to believe.

When Jesus later appeared in the room where the disciples had gathered, He invited Thomas to touch the crucifixion scars. Immediately Thomas declared, "My Lord and My God!" (John 20:28).

When "doubting Thomas" invades our consciousness, we can experience either a hindrance or a boost to our spiritual growth.

A doubt becomes a negative force when we brood over it and pour out our confusion to others. We may even infect them with similar troubling thoughts. Failure to investigate, to lay out the difficulty in prayer, and to use our reasoning powers and other resources contribute to regression rather than growth.

A doubt propels us forward when we treat it as a stepping stone to enlightenment. John the Baptist and Thomas are but two of many people in the Bible who show us that the starting point should always be Christ. His indwelling Spirit will guide us in working through the perplexity. Sometimes we find the answer in Scripture. Sometimes we'll be led to a respected minister, Bible teacher, or Christian writer. Occasionally we may conclude that complete understanding awaits in heaven.

Uncertainty does not signal weak faith. Mature Christians still encounter questions. They also find that a diligent search yields solid knowledge.

✧

My Prayer

Father, keep me turning to You through Your Word and through prayer when I have doubts, and guide me into deeper understanding of biblical truths. Amen.

My Goal

To use doubts and questions about Christianity as a springboard to increasing knowledge.

My Commitment This Week

Choose two or more activities:

____ Give thanks to God for His Word, which is readily available to help me grow in understanding, no matter my age.

____ Write down a question concerning Scripture that troubles me and seek enlightenment through: (1) prayer, (2) the Bible, and (3) a trusted Christian.

____ Read the story of Jesus' encounter with Thomas and the other disciples in John 20:24–31.

____ Visit and pray with a shut-in.

____ Share with another person my new understandings about handling doubts.

✧

9. The Need for Tongue Depressors

Read James 3:1–12

Do not criticize one another. . . .
Whoever criticizes a Christian brother or judges him, criti-
cizes the Law and judges it.
James 4:11, TEV

More than sinusitis caused discomfort as I waited in the doctor's examining room. I was mentally reviewing an earlier conversation with friends when I had sounded off again—breaking my resolve to quit making unkind comments about people.

Then the doctor came in and I began to explain my symptoms. He reached for a tongue depressor, immediately silencing my voice. *Ah,* I thought, *maybe I should carry some of those around to use when I'm poised to be judgmental.*

The practical Book of James describes problems an uncontrolled tongue can produce. The author compares the tongue to a tiny flame that can set a forest ablaze. Thoughtless words damage close relationships and produce lasting rifts in families. Most of us have said things we wish we could take back.

Catherine Marshall wrote about her struggle to overcome a critical nature in *A Closer Walk*, a book drawn from her journals. She said she knew being judgmental was negative and contrary to Jesus' teachings. She said she tried to excuse the weakness on the grounds that one must evaluate situations and people. But on reflection, she rejected this notion and concluded that she was exhibiting a superiority syndrome. She believed this began at an early age, prompted by top grades but the lack of outgoing personality traits that she deeply desired.

Some people say that a judgmental attitude grows out of pride. We know that fault-finding represents a failure to practice Christian love. In the Sermon on the Mount, Jesus spoke about the sin of passing judgment. "With what judgment you judge, you will be judged" (Matt. 7:2).

In our quest for tongue control, our most trusted source of reinforcement is the Holy Spirit. He promises to bolster our weak human nature. Before criticizing another person, if we pause under His guidance to ponder these questions, chances are good that the judgmental comment will die before it springs to life.

✧ Is it true?

✧ Is it hurtful?

✧ Is it necessary?

✧ Does it glorify God?

I memorized these four questions and can attest to their effectiveness. As I am about to pass along a negative opinion, I usually find the second question stops me.

✧

My Prayer

Father, I know it is wrong for me to judge others. Please help me control my tongue. Amen.

My Goal

To refrain from judging other people.

My Commitment This Week

Choose at least two activities:

___ Thank God for the indwelling Holy Spirit who will help me control my tongue.

___ Memorize the checkup questions to apply when I'm poised to express negative judgments.

___ Meditate on 1 Peter 3:8–9. Memorize and post it.

___ Pray the Lord will help me look for the good instead of focusing on the negative side of people and situations.

___ Use a Bible concordance to check for the word *tongue* and copy Scriptures relating to God's teaching on speech habits desirable for a Christian.

10. When Feeling Lonely

Read Matthew 26:36–46

*Then He came to the disciples and found them asleep . . .
"What! Could you not watch with Me one hour?"*
Matthew 26:40

Christians are not immune to loneliness. Nor was our Lord. On the sorrowful night of His betrayal, Christ sought the companionship of three close friends: Peter, James, and John. He asked them to stay and watch with Him at Gethsemane. Yet three times He arose from prayer to find them asleep.

Though surrounded by crowds, Christ was alone on the torturous journey to the cross, where He voluntarily gave up His life. By dying for our sins, He made possible our permanent companionship with God. Our advocate became the Son, who experienced a higher level of loneliness than we can ever know. When He ascended to heaven, He sent the Holy Spirit to indwell us—to comfort and strengthen. On a human level, He pronounced us lifetime members of the family of God.

With the incredible provisions Christ made for us, what would be the best responses at those times when loneliness threatens to envelop us? Scripture suggests two practical steps:

Seek the presence of God. James wrote, "Draw near to God and He will draw near to you" (James 4:8). The more time we spend with God through the Bible and prayer, the better we get to know Him.

Loneliness doesn't cling as tightly to one who takes time for daily fellowship with Him. A woman who lost a loved one said that what helped her most were Scripture suggestions people passed along. Many find the Book of Psalms especially comforting.

Reach out to others. The first commandment is to love God. Jesus said the second is like it. "Love your neighbor as yourself" (Matt. 22:39). A woman told of praying that the Lord would ease her heartache through contacts with others who were lonely. She turned away from her own bleak thoughts as she became absorbed in helping ease the pain of others.

In many communities, Christians are helping to form support groups for those dealing with grief and loneliness. One group shares photographs and talks about loved ones. Neighborhood Bible study often can provide rewarding fellowship as well as provide opportunity for spiritual growth.

Joining others in meaningful church and community work can build rich friendships. Those willing to contribute their talents as the Lord leads are likely to find they not only erase many lonely hours but even must guard against over-commitment.

✧

My Prayer

Father, thank You that I am part of Your family.
Guide me in reaching out to others who may be lonely. Amen.

My Goal

To seek the presence of God in all I do and to reach out to those who may be lonely.

My Commitment This Week

Choose two or more activities:

___ Thank God, that as a Christian, I am never alone, even when I'm without human companionship.

___ Ask God to show me a lonely person to visit. Encourage the person to share stories, using photographs.

___ Read and share *The Path of Loneliness* by Elisabeth Elliott.

___ Read one chapter in 1 John each day during the week. Copy special verses in my notebook.

___ Investigate local opportunities for church or community fellowship and pass the information along to others.

11. Forgiveness

Read Matthew 18:21–35

Be kind to one another, tenderhearted, forgiving one another, even as God in Christ forgave you.
Ephesians 4:32

Several women who had traveled great distances to attend a fiftieth reunion were incensed that one who lived nearby did not make the effort to come.

"It's an insult! I will never forgive her," declared one of the absentee's friends. "And she even wrote and asked me to give her the news about everyone who came."

Any person who says, "I'll never forgive," goes against the teaching of Christ. In the Sermon on the Mount, Jesus stated the consequences of refusing to forgive: "If you forgive others the wrongs they have done to you, your Father in heaven will also forgive you. But if

you do not forgive others, then your Father will not forgive the wrongs you have done" (Matt. 6:14–15, TEV).

Haven't we seen close friendships or family relationships severely strained, if not severed, because of incidents of no more consequence than the missed reunion?
Peter asked Jesus whether seven times was enough to forgive someone. "'No, not seven times,' answered Jesus,
'but seventy times seven.'" (Matt. 18:22, TEV). He made
no distinction between a hurtful slight and a more devastating transgression.

One woman said she could forgive almost anything
except someone who caused physical or mental injury to
a loved one. Corrie ten Boom, that gallant Dutch woman
who served time in a concentration camp during World
War II, faced such a dilemma.

A devout Christian, her faith became even stronger
as she withstood the brutality and indignities of her cap-
tors. Hardest to bear was watching her beloved sister
Betsie succumb to a slow death at Ravensbruck. Following her release in 1944, Corrie ten Boom dedicated her
life to telling others about the love of God.

To her dismay, she was called to speak in a Munich
church. After delivering a message on forgiveness, she
froze as she recognized one of the guards from Ravensbruck making his way toward her. He told her he had become a Christian and that God had forgiven him. "But
will you forgive me?" he asked.

She wrote how a coldness clutched her heart. But she
knew forgiveness was not an emotion but an act of will.
She prayed silently, "I can lift my hand. . . . You supply
the feeling." Mechanically, she thrust her hand into his.
She said, "The current started in my shoulder, raced
down my arm, sprang into our joined hands. Then this
healing warmth seemed to flood my whole being. . . . I
had never known God's love so intensely."

❖

My Prayer

Father, thank You for Your strong love that can fill our hearts and flow out to others in forgiveness, even when we feel cold or resentful. Amen.

My Goal

To forgive others as God in Christ forgives me.

My Commitment This Week

Choose two or more activities:

___ Thank God for His forgiveness of my sins and ask Him to help me forgive "seventy times seven."

___ Ask God to help me recall anyone toward whom I hold a grudge and strengthen me to forgive and forget.

___ Read Psalm 32 as my prayer.

___ Write down, memorize, and use when needed: "I am wrong. I am sorry. I love you. Please forgive me."

___ Ask God to help me talk with family members or friends who say they "can't forgive." Tell them about Corrie ten Boom.

12. Prelude to Prayer

Read John 15:1–8

If you abide in Me, and My words abide in you, you will ask what you desire, and it shall be done for you.
John 15:7

Valuable lessons about prayer were etched in my mind in 1975 when I helped develop a slide presentation for the New York Women's Bible Society. The Society, formed

in 1815 as part of the American Bible Society, was celebrating its 160th anniversary.

A slim budget did not deter Superintendent Grethe
Anderson from setting high standards for the presentation. "It must glorify God," she said, "and capture the audience as much as the best secular production." To
achieve this goal, she prayed about every detail, always
thanking God for what He would do.

As we neared the project's end, I dropped by Grethe's
office to pick her up for lunch and give her an update.
"We've got a super story," I said, as she assembled her papers. "But I regret I don't have time for one more piece of
library research."

"What do you need?" she asked, looking up.

"The story is complete," I said. "But if I had time to
find out about events in New York City when the Bible
Society was founded, it would add an extra dimension."

To my amazement, she smiled broadly, as though I'd
given her good news. "God can handle that," she said.
"We'll pray about it before we go to lunch." She did so,
briefly and specifically.

As we rode down on the elevator, the Bible Society
archivist joined us. She had helped with my records
search. "I'm so glad I ran into you," she said. "In collect-
ing background for a speech our president is giving, I ran
across an essay you might find useful. A profile of New
York City in 1915. All about the politics, economy, and
cultural and religious affairs."

Pondering the incident, I marveled not only at the
immediate answer to prayer, but also at Grethe's confidence that God would give us what we asked. And I realized a gracious Lord had used her to show me two vital
ingredients of effectual prayer.

Abiding in Christ. As with every facet of Grethe's life,
God became chief consultant in the planning and pro-

duction of our anniversary project. So asking for historical information didn't come as an isolated request. We were praying in His will.

Praying specifically. We didn't just pray generally for help. Rather, the request went something like this: "Lord, we need historical facts about New York City to make our project the best it can be. Thank you for helping us get this information."

I soon began to pray about every aspect of my life—in its broad dimensions and in specific details—with great results. Looking back, for example, I see how such abiding in Christ removed all tension from complicated retirement plans.

✧

My Prayer

*Father, increase my ability to abide in You
so that my specific prayers are in Your perfect will. Amen.*

My Goal

To abide in Christ throughout each day.

My Commitment This Week

Choose two or more activities:

___ Read Matthew 6:5–13. List Jesus' prayer pointers.

___ Ask God to help me know Him better and to become more proficient in praying within His will.

___ Bring long-range and immediate concerns to God, thanking Him that He hears and will guide me in His perfect timing.

___ Read and share *What Happens When We Pray for Our Families* by Evelyn Christianson.

___ Pray about joining or starting a small prayer group.

✧

13. A Disturbing Directive

Read Romans 12:9–21

*All Scripture is inspired by God and is useful for teaching the
truth, rebuking error, correcting faults, and giving
instruction for right living.*
2 Timothy 3:16, TEV

"I'm not going to read the Bible any more," announced
an eighty-four-year-old friend who usually reads the
Word daily.

"Why not?" I asked, confident that he didn't mean it,
but curious about what prompted the declaration.

"I don't like what it tells me to do," he replied. I
couldn't help smiling when I learned that the biblical instructions he received related to a fence he was putting on
his property that was annoying a neighbor. Since the
neighbor had treated my friend unfairly on several occa-
sions, I had sympathized when he told me earlier about
his decision not to alter his plans. What he was doing
broke no property laws.

"It's very plain," he said, "there in the twelfth and
thirteenth chapters of Romans. Look for yourself."

Opening the Bible to Romans 12, I saw clearly the
message that had convicted him: "Be kindly affection-
ate to one another with brotherly love, in honor giving
preference to one another" (v. 10). "Repay no one evil
for evil" (v. 17). "Do not avenge yourselves. 'Vengeance
is Mine. I will repay,' says the Lord" (v. 19). And in
Romans 13:10: "Love does no harm to a neighbor;
therefore love is the fulfillment of the law."

Dwight Moody once said that the Bible was not giv-
en to increase our knowledge but to change our lives. The
more diligently we saturate our minds with Scripture and

obey its instructions, the more likely our lives are to conform to what God wants them to be.

Too many Christians, regular church-goers among them, say they can't get anything out of Bible reading. Experience will show that the best way to solve this problem is to pray before beginning, asking the Holy Spirit to help make the message clear and applicable to life. Sometimes difficult passages may need to be put aside for a time. Most people find that as a new truth becomes plain, they eagerly seek to learn more.

My neighbor taught me an important lesson about obedience. I walked out when I saw him moving the fence. "God showed me a better idea," he said, grinning broadly. "If I do it this way, the privacy is better, which is what I was after. And my neighbor will be happy."

He continues his daily Bible reading.

✧

My Prayer

Father, thank You for speaking to us plainly from Your Word. Help me to understand and act on Your instructions given there. Amen.

My Goal

To saturate my mind daily with Scripture and obey what it tells me to do.

My Commitment This Week

Choose two or more activities:

___ Set aside a time to read the Bible daily.

___ Ask God to help me understand what I read and to impress on my mind actions I should take.

___ Ask God to stop me if I am about to do something contrary to biblical teaching.

___ Join a small Bible study group where I can discuss the meaning of Scripture with others.

___ Visit a Christian bookstore and examine new translations of the Bible that are easier to read and those that include study notes.

14. Worship as a Partnership

Read Psalm 122

I was glad when they said to me, "Let us go into the house of the LORD."
Psalm 122:1

"Wasn't that a wonderful sermon!"

"I might as well have stayed home and read the paper for all I got out of that sermon!"

Most of us have heard and maybe voiced such diverse opinions during our many decades of church-going. The sermon *is* the centerpiece of Sunday worship. But something a Baptist minister said to me several years ago changed the way I view a worship service. He spoke of his frustration with those who felt that all was well if they made it to church before the sermon.

"How can I convince them the sermon is only part of worship?" he asked. "And that if they participated fully, there are times they'd get more from other parts of the service than from my preaching?"

Applying his comments to myself, I began to pray for guidance in achieving more meaningful involvement. Gradually, I sensed God illuminating five practical steps:

Prepare for worship. Begin early Sunday morning during private devotions. Ask God to clear distractions so you can focus heart and mind on Him. Lift up the service and those leading and attending.

Preview Scripture. Try to be in the pew ten or fifteen minutes early for quiet meditation. Read the Bible passages noted in the bulletin. Compare "your" message with the minister's teaching.

Multiply musical blessings. Singing lifts our spirits, but a bonus follows when we make a conscious effort to absorb the words of hymns. Many are Scriptures set to music. You may receive a fresh reminder of God's awesome power. Perhaps you will enjoy the comfort of a beautifully phrased promise of His to claim.

Join in pastoral prayers. Pray with the minister, silently echoing words of adoration and thanksgiving, and agreeing with intercessions for people and situations. Such participation expands horizons of concern and helps you keep focused on God.

Expect a "take-away" from the sermon. Ask God to impress on you at least one personal message—something to take action about or to share. Such expectant listening produces quite different results than when you tend to wait passively, silently challenging the minister to capture your attention. Fruitful worship is a partnership.

As I follow these steps, asking God to help me refrain from slipping back into judgmental attitudes, my Sunday morning worship boosts my spiritual growth.

✧

My Prayer

Father, help me become more diligent in worship
so your message takes root and bears fruit. Amen.

My Goal

To become more personally involved in Sunday worship.

My Commitment This Week

Choose two or more activities:

___ During worship ask God for a message from Scripture, hymns, and the sermon. Join silently in prayers.

___ Pray for the minister each day, that God will provide wisdom and guidance during sermon preparation.

___ Meditate on Psalm 84. Give thanks for my church.

___ Read 2 Chronicles 5 about the joyous worship service when the ark was brought to the temple.

___ Read Psalm 95. Memorize verses 6–7.

✧

15. First Impressions Last

Read Colossians 3:12–17

We also pray that your outward lives, which men see, may bring credit to your master's name.
Colossians 1:10, PHILLIPS

"How did you happen to come to Good Samaritan?" I asked a couple who moved into the retirement village where I live.

"A few years ago we were on a bus tour with some folks from here," replied Frances. "They were fun to travel with. We liked them. And they talked about what a nice place this was to live."

"Having made the decision to move into a retirement community, we decided to investigate this one," added her husband Joe.

The enthusiastic residents had obviously made a lasting impression during their brief acquaintance with the couple, causing them to investigate. The couple liked what they saw, eventually becoming residents themselves.

Reflecting on the incident, I wondered if it provided a good pattern for the everyday lives of Christians. Could my life radiate such joy in being a part of the family of God that others would be motivated to investigate? Feeling inadequate to lead people to Christ, could I be one part of the process?

Hannah Whitall Smith, whose books on the Christian life have become classics, wrote how she was visiting with an intelligent agnostic whom she wished to influence. He listened politely for a while and then said, "If you Christians want to make us agnostics inclined to look at your religion, you must be more comfortable in it. The Christians I meet seem to me to be the most uncomfortable people around. I, for one, do not care to have that sort of religion."

The Bible offers much guidance about how to be "comfortable" in our religion. In the third chapter of Colossians, Paul told believers that once we belong to Christ we can live a "new life." Energized by His power as we successfully follow these directives of Paul, our lives will reflect attitudes and actions that appeal to others.

Cultivate a heart of compassion, so we exhibit tolerance, patience, kindness, humility, and forgiveness.

Strive to eliminate all wrong attributes, such as anger, an evil temper, lies, filthy language, envy, and immorality.

Be truly loving, which the *Phillip's* translation describes as "the golden chain of all virtues" (Col. 3:14). Tom Landry, a prominent Texan and first coach of the Dallas Cowboys, is one who radiates comfort with Christianity. He expresses love by putting God first, family second, others next, and himself last.

Let thankfulness permeate your actions, and whatever you do, do heartily as to the Lord.

Following these directives under Christ's power will produce transformed lives that God can use.

My Prayer

Father, empower me to follow Paul's instructions so that my life reflects joy and comfort in being a Christian. Amen.

My Goal

To live so people know God comes first in my life.

My Commitment This Week

Choose two or more activities:

___ Analyze my behavior against the four directives, asking God to help me change where I should.

___ Ask God daily to help me act and speak in ways that reflect my joy and "comfort" in being a Christian.

___ Read Colossians 3 to review rules for holy living.

___ Substitute a smile and "Have a blessed day" instead of the traditional "Have a good day."

___ Ask God to give me one person with whom to discuss my faith.

16. Grapes and Giants

Read Numbers 14:6–10

*If the L*ORD *delights in us, then He will bring us into this land and give it to us.*
Numbers 14:8

When Moses was camped with the Israelites in the wilderness, the Lord told him to spy out Canaan, the promised land. Moses sent one leader from each of the twelve tribes, instructing them to see whether the inhabitants were strong or weak, many or few. He also told them to check out the land itself to determine whether it was fertile or poor and to bring out some of the fruit.

After forty days of exploration, the twelve spies returned, bringing a huge cluster of grapes on a pole between two men. The scouts were unanimous in their euphoria over the rich land, attested to in part by the grapes and other fruit they brought. The land truly "flowed with milk and honey," as the Lord had promised when He led them out of Egypt.

Yet on the matter of the inhabitants of Canaan, two sharply different reports were voiced. Caleb, supported by Joshua, urged the group to push forward and take the land. Caleb's confidence sprang from his trust in the Lord's ability to protect and direct them, in spite of the opposition. The negative assessment of the majority, however, soon plunged the Israelites into total gloom. The ten described the cities as large and well fortified. "The people were big and strong, like giants," they claimed. "We were like grasshoppers beside them."

The Israelites began complaining and lamenting the fact that they hadn't died in the wilderness, saying they would be better off returning to Egypt. They spoke of stoning Caleb and Joshua.

Upset by their lack of trust, God decreed that the chosen people must wander in the desert another forty years—until that generation perished. Only Joshua and Caleb survived. Joshua became leader when Moses died. Caleb's faith was rewarded when he and his descendants were given the parcel of land he had scouted.

This story of fear and faith remains as relevant today as at the time of the Exodus, especially for older adults. As Paul reminded Timothy, the spirit of fear does not come from God. Rather, fear activates the power of Satan, keeping us stirred up and uneasy, increasing the size of our foes. Faith, however, activates the power of God, diminishing the size of giants—whether in the guise of health problems, money concerns, broken relationships, or something else.

✧

My Prayer

Father, increase my faith so that it wipes out fears that threaten to engulf me in my remaining years. Amen.

My Goal

To attain a faith that trusts God and banishes fear.

My Commitment This Week

Choose two or more activities.

___ Thank God for the faith He has given me.

___ Thank God for His faithfulness in caring for me in the past and for the way He will do so in the future.

___ Identify fears hovering over me, and ask God to expel them while guiding me in actions I should take, if any.

___ Check the word *fear* in a Bible concordance. Look up verses and copy those that are meaningful to me.

___ Share Scriptures copied with a fearful person.

✧

17. Mastering the Owner's Manual

Read Luke 24:44–49

Then he opened their minds so they could understand the Scriptures.
Luke 24:45, NIV

God not only gave believers a "how-to" manual for daily living; He also provided a Counselor to help us understand and act on the information presented. Yet countless church members confess that they get little or no enlightenment when they read the Bible. Sadly, it remains unopened even by many Christians.

"I know I should read it," said a friend in her seventies, "but I don't get anything out of it."

"Maybe I shouldn't admit this," said another, "but I just get sleepy if I try to read the Bible."

I empathize with both comments, since I was well into middle age before I recognized what had hindered my personal Bible study and halted my spiritual growth at a kindergarten level for many decades. In answer to prayer, God guided me into these four steps that began to unlock Scripture and help me apply its principles to my own life.

Seek supernatural guidance. Jesus promised His disciples that when He ascended to heaven, the Father would send a Counselor, the Holy Spirit, who "will teach you all things" (John 14:26).

Paul says that human wisdom and desire aren't enough. We need the Holy Spirit linked to our spirit to help us understand the Scriptures, and to provide us with know-how and power to obey God's directives.

Study systematically, asking questions. A study Bible with subheads may be helpful. First, read through a book in the Bible to get an overview and learn its major theme. Think about the author, time, and audience. Then go back and read each short chapter or sections of longer chapters, trying to discover answers to questions such as: Who is speaking? Can I summarize the incident or message? What does God want me to learn from it? How does the message apply to today?

Explore personal application. What actions should I try to imitate? What promises from God can I claim?

What attitudes hidden in me need correction? Is a sin pointed to that I need to confess? Is a prayer suggested for others or myself? What information remains unclear, that I must accept by faith until further enlightenment?

Use other aids. Most people find that a notebook is helpful for writing down new insights as they read. A Bible dictionary, handbook, and commentary may be useful. Ask God to give you a study partner or small group where you explore questions.

If new to personal Bible study, reading may be slow at first. Persistence pays. As you rely on the Holy Spirit, you will begin to sense God giving you special insights.

My Prayer

Father, help me get into Your Word, so Your Word gets into me and my life reflects what You want it to be. Amen.

My Goal

To better understand and apply biblical teachings.

My Commitment This Week

Choose two or more activities:

___ Ask God to guide me as I seek more effective Bible study.

___ Explore the study aids suggested in this meditation. (*What the Bible Is All About* by Henrietta Mears has helped many.)

___ Meditate on and memorize 2 Timothy 3:16–17.

___ Select a specific time and place for daily Bible study. Be faithful in keeping this important appointment.

___ Follow the four steps suggested in this meditation, adding others as I find them helpful.

18. Images to Keep

Read 2 Peter 1:10–15

I will be careful to ensure that you always have a reminder of these things after my decease.
2 Peter 1:15

"The only thing I don't like about living in a retirement village is making new friends and having them die," confessed a friend.

We had lost several in our Village family recently, so on one level I understood her sentiments. But I searched unsuccessfully for words to explain why, for me, the joys of friendships, however brief, overshadow the sadness of earthly good-byes. How exciting then, to hear the feelings I wanted to express, beautifully articulated by the minister who conducted the service celebrating the life of my friend Leonard.

"Leonard was securely anchored to his faith," said the minister. "He loved life but understood death and even welcomed it. He knew he was a fortunate person to live eighty-seven years and to have sixty-six years in a loving marriage." Then the minister spoke of the "treasures left for family and friends in the form of images of his life which reflect God's beauty and truth, images to hang on the walls of our hearts and minds—of ranching, kindnesses to strangers, smiles, laughter, courage, and steadiness in the storm."

As I contemplated the many positive images left by Leonard, I also rejoiced in those of others I've been blessed to count as friends during my few years at Good Samaritan Village. I believe I'm a better person for having witnessed their faith, love, joy, and courage in action.

I remember how Mary continued to focus actions and thoughts on others, even as weakness and pain worsened during her last weeks. Sam, tall and dignified in his crisp candy-striped jacket, volunteered many hours in the Village Shop, dispensing good humor and encouragement along with groceries.

I recall frequent mid-morning teatime with Effie when we shared experiences about our faith and families. And Louise, after losing her beloved husband of over six decades, comforted many by hosting an evening fellowship hour in her apartment. "We cry a little," she told me, "but we laugh a lot too."

These friends prompted me to make two resolutions: *to participate in life to the fullest*, giving thanks for the opportunities for new friendships, spiritual and cultural enrichment, fun, and service to others; and *to organize my affairs*, so as to gain a new sense of peace about my own mortality, and be ready when God calls me.

✧

My Prayer

Father, thank You for friends. Guide me so that the images I leave will be positive ones—to You and to my family and friends. Amen.

My Goal

To live so the images I leave behind will glorify God.

My Commitment This Week

Choose two or more activities:

___ Recall those who inspired me and enriched my life. Give thanks to God for them by name.

___ Read Scripture portions about heaven, such as John 14:1–6; Philippians 1:21–23; 2 Timothy 4:6–8; and Revelation 21–22.

___ Read *A Grief Observed* by C. S. Lewis, and share it with a friend who is grieving.

___ Pray about how to organize my affairs so I will be ready when God is ready for me. Take the first step.

___ Spend the day with someone who has lost a loved one in the last year.

19. Activating God's Gifts

Read 1 Peter 4:7–11

Each one should use whatever gift he has received . . .
faithfully administering God's grace in its various forms.
1 Peter 4:10, NIV

The multi-gifted Delany sisters, authors at ages 105 and 103 of the 1994 *Book of Everyday Wisdom,* grew up in a family of 10 children, where the Bible and prayer guided daily life. Their parents established the motto "to help someone" and taught it in part through example.

The motto became firmly rooted and the women remained alert to opportunities to implement it throughout their lives. For example, a young boy helping them with chores couldn't bring himself to look at them. He would stare at the ground, hunching his shoulders and mumbling. They took him on as a project, encouraging him to stand up straight, speak clearly, and look them "directly in the eye."

"It took awhile to break him of his habits," they wrote, "but the change was amazing. His voice got louder. His enunciation improved. His confidence grew." Finally, he confirmed the success of their efforts. He came over standing proud and tall, and in a strong voice, looking one of the sisters straight in the eye, made an offer: "For a dollar I'll feed your dog every day. But all I'll do is feed him. I won't wash the dish."

This extraordinary use of the gift of encouragement by people past one hundred inspires us to examine our own actions. Are we developing and using our talents? The Bible says we've all received one or more gifts. Retirement years usually release time to increase their use. Consider these "starter" ideas:

Encouragement can be activated in many ways, including helping a young person develop, as the Delany sisters did. Most of us could do this.

Hospitality can be exhibited through our car or our home as we dedicate these possessions to God's use. For many, food becomes a tangible expression of neighborliness. A friend with a VCR rents videos and invites people over.

Service cuts across many areas, including hospitals and other health care facilities, schools, youth involvement activities, adult centers, "Meals on Wheels," soup kitchens, and much more.

Creative skills can soar into fulfilling second careers as artists, wood-carvers, silversmiths, musicians, or writers. Many pursue needlework or gardening. In sharing results or teaching others, joy envelops creator and receiver.

Even if health problems slow us down, God can help us spend time and resources in ways that benefit others. Intercessory prayer offers a way all can serve.

✧

My Prayer

Father, help me activate the gifts You have given me in ways that bless others and glorify You. Amen.

My Goal

To use the gifts God has given me to accomplish His purpose for me for the rest of my life.

My Commitment This Week

Choose two or more activities:

____ Ask God to help me recognize and make the best use of the talents He has given me.

____ Examine my use of time and decide whether I have a good balance of work, family needs, play, and service.

____ Explore volunteer needs in line with my talents.

____ Write a letter of encouragement to a young person.

____ Read 1 Corinthians 12. Ask God to show me how I can best contribute to His body, the church.

20. The Noisy Psalm

Read Psalm 46

Be still, and know that I am God.
Psalm 46:10

As I read the wild upheavals described in Psalm 46—roaring waters, shaking mountains, raging nations, and burning chariots—I became aware of God the Creator in charge of history. Yet above the turbulence, I also see the God of the individual. This psalm inspired Martin Luther's great hymn, "A Mighty Fortress Is Our God."

Immersing yourself in this powerful psalm will calm fears and ease weariness, loneliness, helplessness, and sorrow. Called the "song of confidence," it captures the essence of faith without ever using the word. The message encompasses three promises made to those who put their trust in the Heavenly Father.

His power, summarized succinctly in the opening verse, "God is our refuge and strength, a very present help in trouble." In light of such assurance, fear fades into faith, if we permit it. No matter what storm rages, His strength can envelop our weakness. When the apostle Paul prayed to have a physical handicap removed, the Lord said that His grace was enough, that His power was shown the more completely in weakness.

His presence, confirmed in a refrain repeated in the psalm: "The Lord of Hosts is with us; the God of Jacob is our refuge." Herein springs our confidence—the consciousness of the presence of God, no matter the tumult around. Writing to the Romans, Paul put it this way: "There is nothing in all creation that will ever be able to separate us from the love of God which is ours through Christ Jesus our Lord" (Rom. 8:39, TEV).

His peace, graciously offered through the invitation to "Be still and know" in the midst of the earthly desolation described in the psalm. Such peace was evident in a man who lost his wife in the 1995 Oklahoma bombing disaster when he said, "God is good. He gives you strength to do what you have to do."

Paul reminded believers, "Don't worry about anything, but in all your prayers ask God for what you need, always asking him with a thankful heart" (Phil. 4:6, TEV). They were promised that if they did so, the peace of God, which is beyond human ability to understand, would fill their hearts and minds. Countless Christians who have known God's peace attest to the validity of this advice.

❖

My Prayer

Father, thank You for Your Word, which confirms again and again that You are my refuge and strength and a constant help no matter what troubles arise. Help me to be still and experience Your presence. Amen.

My Goal

To learn to "be still" and experience God's presence and His peace even in the midst of troubles.

My Commitment This Week

Choose two or more activities:

___ Ask God to help me accomplish my goal of experiencing His presence each day.

___ Pray for wisdom for our national, state, and local government leaders.

___ Pray about any personal situation that concerns me, asking for God's guidance and expecting His peace.

___ Read Psalm 46 each day, using different translations.

___ Read the words of the hymn "A Mighty Fortress Is Our God," personalizing it by substituting "my" for "our" and "I" for "we." Ask God to help me absorb the powerful message.

21. Left-Hand Miracle

Read Romans 8:25–39

His Spirit within us is actually praying for us in those agonizing longings which never find words.
Romans 8:26, PHILLIPS

"I wanted to pray but I couldn't," said my brother Ray. "God seemed dim and far away. I didn't know how to reach Him."

The experience he described took place following a stroke that produced a two-week coma, left his right side permanently paralyzed, and impaired his ability to think and speak. Though only fifty-six, he was forced to liquidate his car dealership and give up favorite Colorado pastimes: skiing and trout fishing.

A devout Christian, Ray had launched each day with a fifteen-minute quiet time in his office. He participated in Gideon International, a Bible study/prayer group, and other church activities. During months of therapy, the fog in his brain slowly lifted, only to be replaced by the terrifying thought of replacing his active lifestyle with a sedentary one.

"A dream began taking shape in my head," he said, "so farfetched that at first I didn't even tell my wife." It involved a recent hobby, silversmithing. Though right-handed, could he manage the craft with only the left one? If so, he would have something productive to do. Knowing nothing was impossible with God, he went to work to make his dream a reality.

Setbacks overshadowed gains at first. Yet even dismal results with occupational therapy propelled him forward as he saw people in worse condition. He set up shop in a small bedroom and made a second "hand" from vises, clamps, and clothespins.

The stroke had interrupted Ray's work on a wedding gift, a silver-and-copper plaque of "The Last Supper." He said if he could finish it, "that would be God's sign I could make it as a one-armed craftsman." Soon he was sawing tiny silver heads of the apostles. Work progressed slowly and awkwardly, but each small victory energized him for the next step. With the mailing of the gift, his dream came to life!

He immediately started a plaque for the church in gratitude for prayers and kindnesses. As Ray created more aids to produce more intricate work, his shop took on a Rube Goldberg look. The quality and quantity of his output—including squash blossom necklaces, pins, pendants, and other jewelry—attest to his high standards and perseverance. His creations number more than 700 (including 80 Last Supper plaques), given away, or made to order and sold. Now in his seventies, he has designed and produced working models of windmills, oil drilling rigs, and the California Cable Car system.

Ray confirms God's faithfulness as he still puts difficult problems before Him. He is even going fly-fishing again.

✧

My Prayer

Father, thank You for answering the deep longings of my heart even when words fail. Amen.

My Goal

To trust God for the impossible dream while doing all I can to achieve it.

My Commitment This Week

Choose two or more activities:

___ Thank God for His Spirit within, who prays for me when words don't come.

___ Ask God to help me persevere with difficult tasks.

___ Ask God to impress on my mind any new thing He wants me to accomplish this week.

___ Ask God to help me encourage a handicapped person.

___ Read all stanzas of "How Firm a Foundation." Make a list of the biblical promises there.

✧

22. R$_x$: Laughter

Read Proverbs 17:17–24

A merry heart does good, like medicine.
Proverbs 17:22

This biblical truth concerning the medicinal effects of laughter was chronicled by Norman Cousins in his book *Anatomy of an Illness*. At the time, he suffered from a painful disease that involved severe inflammation of the spine and joints. He discovered that ten minutes of solid laughter would give him two hours of pain-free sleep. Funny movies and books, and tapes of comics provided his main amusement aids.

Physicians became so intrigued that they tested his sedimentation rate (which measures inflammation or infection) before and after periods of robust laughter. They found results positive and cumulative.

Cousins emphasized two elements as being central in battling serious illness. First, patients must obtain the best that medical science can contribute. Second, patients must willingly summon all their physical and spiritual resources to help fight the disorder. He said,

> Hope, faith, love, humor, and a strong will to live offer no promise of immortality, only proof of our uniqueness as human beings and the opportunity to experience full growth even under the grimmest circumstances. Far more real than the ticking of time is the way we open up the minutes and invest them with meaning. . . . The ultimate tragedy is to die without discovering the possibilities of full growth.

A retired teacher serving as a hospice volunteer told of a unique assignment with Chuck, a patient dying of cancer. Though often weak and in pain, Chuck delighted in entertaining his new visitor with funny stories from his "checkered past." His quick wit charmed the volunteer, a compassionate listener, and the two men established a bond that prompted lengthy sessions together. When not visiting face to face, they often talked by phone. Apologetic for taking so much of his friend's time, Chuck said, "I just don't hurt as much when I'm talking to you."

One day the hospice nurse stopped by to give Chuck a good news/bad news report. "The bad news—your six months hospice coverage has run out because you outlived your doctor's prognosis," she said. "The good news—your volunteer says his visits will continue."

"I should certainly hope so!" exclaimed Chuck. "He's what's keeping me alive."

✧

My Prayer

Father, create a happy heart in me, and open its windows so Your radiance may escape and serve as a soothing balm to those I meet who are hurting in mind or body. Amen.

My Goal

To enlist God's help in increasing my ability to use humor when appropriate to benefit others and myself.

My Commitment This Week

Choose two or more activities:

___ Ask God to help me maintain a cheerful outlook, and use wholesome humor to benefit others or myself.

___ Read and share the book *Head First: the Biology of Hope* by Norman Cousins.

___ Visit someone who is ill, asking God to guide my speech so that it is appropriate to the person's condition.

___ Give an amusing book to someone who is lonely. Get suggestions at a Christian bookstore.

___ Pray about whether to train to become a volunteer in hospice or another health care agency.

23. Celebrate Life's Extras

Read Genesis 1:9–14

Consider the lilies of the field . . . even Solomon in all his glory was not arrayed like one of these.
Matthew 6:28–29

My neighbor across the street called one August morning with a surprising query. "I wondered whether you had taken a good look at the crepe myrtle in your front yard," he said. I had not. "You need to go look at them. They're beautiful. I'm really enjoying my view."

Health problems hinder my neighbor's mobility; but I think his powers of observation, appreciation, and thoughtfulness have been heightened. He sent a visiting daughter over with snapshots of my flowering shrubs.

I turned to the writings of Archibald Rutledge, Poet Laureate of South Carolina. He was said to "see sermons in stones and books in brooks and the bright light of God over everything." He wrote about the deeply spiritual extras for seekers to find in the bottomless bounty of nature. To him they represent the handiwork and love of God. He said extras have brought "so clear a consciousness of God that of all men the atheist appears to me the most pitiable and foolish."

Rutledge told of visiting a very sick friend one October night: "There was a full moon; as I walked down the village street on my sad mission I felt the silvery beauty of it quiet my heart. The world lay lustrous. There was no scrawny bush nor ugly clod that was not transfigured. . . . A little breeze over the salt tide brought aromatic marshy odors."

His friend also felt the beauty from his window and delighted in the odors brought in by the breeze. The melody of a mockingbird charmed them.

Poets help us appreciate afresh how God enriches our lives through nature—far beyond the necessities of existence. If we reach into our memory banks, most of us can extract images that attest to the awesome perfection of the Creator's handiwork. Photographs help us hold on to our mental pictures for our own continued enjoyment and to share with others.

But photographs don't capture the stirring of the soul produced by a majestic forest in Washington, a clear rippling stream in Colorado, or a medley of wild flowers dazzling a gray ribbon of Texas highway.

And thanks to my neighbor, I now savor clusters of delicate pink crepe myrtle blossoms viewed behind the lightning-seared trunk of a sprawling mesquite tree in my front yard. I also watch with joy when a little hummingbird joins a bevy of bees feasting on the flowering bushes outside my back window. Often I stand in awe, gazing on the perfection of a blazing sunset.

✧

My Prayer

Father, this week, open my eyes afresh to absorb the glorious extras you provide that beautify our lives. Amen.

My Goal

To look with new eyes at the wonder of God's creation.

My Commitment This Week

Choose at least two activities

___ Look around and thank God each day for a different aspect of nature that enriches our lives.

___ Examine a single flower with a child, explaining that God made it. Explore other evidences of His handiwork.

___ Read and share *Life's Extras* by Archibald Rutledge.

___ Make the hymn "For the Beauty of the Earth" my prayer.

___ Invite someone for a scenic drive.

24. A Polish Mother's Prayer

Read Luke 22: 31–34

But I have prayed for you, that your faith should not fail.
Luke 22:32

A special danger hovered over Peter. Satan, out to destroy him, had asked God for permission to "sift" him like wheat. Jesus not only prayed for Peter but lovingly told him so.

Some years ago, before modern heart surgery techniques, a special danger hovered over George, a thirty-year-old Polish man. Lying in a hospital bed in Detroit, he was waiting for an operation to open a severely obstructed aortic valve.

A relatively new instrument, a dilator, was being used. Precisely placed and activated, the tiny dilator was designed to break up the calcification in the valve so blood could flow into the aorta. The procedure was difficult and risky, however.

When my brother, Dr. Conrad Lam, visited the patient the afternoon before surgery, his mother was sitting by the bedside. She spoke only Polish. At one point she said something to her son. He told the doctor, "My mother wants you to know she will go to the church at 6:00 A.M. and will be praying until noon."

The next morning, the first stages of the surgery progressed smoothly. But the instrument could not be maneuvered through the calcium deposits on the valve so that the dilator head could reach the aorta. The surgeon tried repeatedly, but to no avail.

In spite of a blood transfusion, the anesthetist began to call attention to dangerously low blood pressure. With the patient's heart beating feebly, Dr. Lam reluctantly removed the dilator. He applied sutures and then asked an assisting physician to close the chest.

As Dr. Lam stripped off his gloves, he glanced at the clock. It was 10:30. A vision of the Polish mother praying at the church filled his mind. She had now been praying four and a half hours. "Well, I'll just have to tell her that because of the calcium on George's valve, her prayers were futile," he said to himself. Then suddenly he asked a nurse for fresh gown and gloves. He quickly scrubbed up and resumed his place among the astonished surgical team. "We're going to try again," he said.

By then another unit of blood had been transfused and the heart action was better. He inserted the instrument and quickly recognized it had reached the right place. He compressed the dilator handles and the sound of the crack reverberated off the operating room walls!

During the surgeon's postoperative visit, the patient's beaming mother held her son's hand. Again she gave him a message to translate. "She wants to thank you for saving my life."

"Please give her *my* best thanks," replied the doctor. "Her prayers were a very important part."

✧

My Prayer

Father, thank You for the skilled and caring health care teams; and thank You for hearing our prayers for them. Amen.

My Goal

To pray for family and friends who have health problems, and for physicians and others caring for them.

My Commitment This Week

Choose two or more activities:

___ Ask God to continue to attract caring men and women to the medical and health care professions.

___ Pray for the Lord's guidance for the medical team caring for a family member or friend. (If possible, let them know it.)

___ Take a tape—sermon, Scripture, or hymns—to a shut-in.

___ Sit with a patient while the caregiver takes a break.

___ Visit and pray with someone scheduled for surgery.

✧

25. What's in a Name?

Read Isaiah 9:1–7

His name will be called Wonderful, Counselor, Mighty God, Everlasting Father, Prince of Peace.
Isaiah 9:6

"Wife, mother, grandmother, daughter, Bible teacher, writer, and friend," said the woman as she introduced a luncheon speaker. "And she excels in all of those roles." All of us fulfill different roles depending on our relationship with a person or group. Most of us perform some roles more effectively than others.

The titles used in the Bible for Christ illuminate an infinite number of roles, all performed to perfection. I once received an intriguing Christmas card featuring an attractive design incorporating twenty-five names for Him. With the Bible as reference, one could easily double the list.

Each title reflects a characteristic of the Person and work of Jesus Christ. To fully identify the only perfect Person to live among us—totally man, totally God—remains impossible. Yet exploring titles from Isaiah and other Scripture provides fresh insights about the incredible Man who wants to guide us daily.

Wonderful might be expressed in today's language as *marvelous, extraordinary, amazing, fantastic, phenomenal* when applied to Christ's actions on behalf of those who claim Him as Savior.

Counselor summarizes His position as Guide, Advisor, Confidant and Tutor to be called on during life's ups and downs. When linked with "wonderful" we glimpse the help He promises.

Mighty God denotes ultimate power and majesty, the King of kings and Lord of lords, a commanding presence for whom "nothing will be impossible" (Luke 1:37).

Everlasting Father describes His status as supernatural Parent to us, imperishable, enduring, permanent, One who provides eternal life because of what He accomplished through His Son.

Prince of Peace suggests that His righteousness will ultimately prevail over the world and also permeate the depths of each believer's heart.

Teacher and Master (Rabboni!) expressed Mary Magdalene's recognition of Christ when He spoke to her at the empty tomb on Easter morning.

"*The Lamb of God* who takes away the sin of the world!" (John 1:29) proclaimed John the Baptist when he first saw Jesus walking toward him.

Messiah (the Anointed One of God) was how Jesus identified Himself to the Samaritan woman at the well.

These names and others help define our Savior. The apostle Paul reminded us that, "God also has highly exalted Him and given Him a name which is above every name . . . that every tongue should confess that Jesus Christ is Lord" (Phil. 2:9, 11).

✧

My Prayer

Father, thank You for Your love, in all its incredible dimensions, that is ours to live by and share. Amen.

My Goal

To try to get better acquainted with the amazing Man who is my Savior.

My Commitment This Week

Choose two or more activities:

___ Give thanks for Christ, my Savior, asking God to help me know Him better. Share my knowledge.

___ Enlist one or more friends to make lists of names for Jesus. Meet and discuss our findings.

___ Take the list with me when I visit a shut-in or a Bible group. Explore the names together, adding others.

___ List names for the roles I play in my family, church, and community. Pray about any I need to perform better.

___ Make the words of the hymn "O for a Thousand Tongues to Sing" my prayer.

26. Complaint Control

Read Numbers 11:1–6

Now when the people complained, it displeased the Lord . . .
and His anger was aroused.
Numbers 11:1

"I've made my own decisions for more than sixty years and I don't like her telling me what to do!" complained a friend about someone we both knew and admired. "Why does she always try to run things?"

While I tried to formulate a reply that might temper her resentment, she continued, the edge in her voice subdued. "I guess I just have to pray for patience again."

"Good solution," I said. I understood her frustration, but my study of the forty-year trek of the Israelites impressed on me God's anger toward complainers.

Soon after the chosen people experienced the spectacular deliverance from captivity, they began grumbling to Moses and Aaron about the hardships of travel. God provided water and food and demonstrated His power and holy attributes in other ways. Yet short memories and weak faith repeatedly plunged them into trouble. Supplied with manna, they craved cucumbers and leeks instead of thanking God for His provisions.

At the border of Canaan, a land that twelve spies confirmed as lush and fertile, the people refused to enter. Ten of the spies complained about the strength of the inhabitants.

Ignoring the two spies who insisted God would give victory, the Israelites discussed selecting a new leader to take them back to Egypt. Only the earnest prayer of Moses prevented God from disinheriting them. God punished them, however, by leaving them in the desert until "the carcasses of you who have murmured against Me shall fall" (Num. 14:29).

As in Moses' day, complaining easily becomes habit-forming. Our sinful nature readily slides into reciting wrongs instead of applauding the good. Further, we can infect others with our negativism. When someone in a group began grumbling about income taxes, most of us joined in. Then one woman convicted us with a quiet comment: "I'm so thankful to have enough income to pay taxes."

Gratitude represents a good antidote for a complaining spirit. We often see such response in the wake of natural disasters that strike communities. I saw it when a friend lost her eyesight after her husband lost his hearing. "We are so fortunate," she said. "He can be my eyes and I can be his ears."

The apostle Paul gave us a worthy goal: "Do all things without murmuring and disputing, that you may become . . . children of God without fault in a crooked and perverse generation" (Phil. 2: 14–15).

✧

My Prayer

Father, help me substitute thanks to You
for the complaints that surface too readily. Amen.

My Goal

To refrain from complaining, giving thanks instead.

My Commitment This Week

Choose two or more activities:
___ Ask God to help me refrain from complaining.

___ Ask God to help me cultivate a habit of gratitude for every aspect of my life, mindful that He is in charge.

___ Make a list of anything negative that surfaces during the week and write down blessings arising from it.

___ Ask God to help me react to complaints expressed by others by mentioning a blessing connected to each.

___ Read Numbers 14, describing God's anger toward the complaining Israelites and Moses' prayer.

27. Love

Read 1 Corinthians 13

And now abide faith, hope, love, these three;
but the greatest of these is love.
1 Corinthians 13:13

Love, the greatest of Christian virtues, defies clear definition. Even the Bible doesn't define it but rather lists its attributes (such as patience, endurance, long-suffering, kindness) and suggests ways to put love into action. The New Testament presents it as the mainspring of holy living.

God in His very nature and essence *is* love, and through His Holy Spirit, He gives believers the ability to love Him and one another. Christianity remains unique among religions in this respect.

John 3:16 may be so familiar that it deserves a fresh look at how it puts divine—active—love in perspective: "God so loved the world that He gave His only begotten Son."

Jesus, the earthly personification of God's love, was asked by a lawyer to name the greatest commandment. He said: "'You shall love the Lord your God with all your heart'. . . . And the second, like it, is this: 'You shall love your neighbor as yourself'" (Mark 12:30–31).

The first of these commandments strikes me as even more awesome than the second. We *want* to love God with our whole being—not only because He commands it but also because of His incredible goodness to us. But the "how to" mystifies us. I learned early in my spiritual journey that the Counselor, the Holy Spirit, whom God sends to every believer, will help *if* I ask. In the matter of love, I sense two broad directives.

Spend time alone with God. For most of us, retirement provides an opportunity to schedule quality quiet time to meet with Him. The goal: to get to know Him in an increasingly personal way. Not just know *about* Him, as we might learn through Sunday School, sermons, religious books, and fellowship with other Christians—as rewarding as these activities are. Even as satisfying friendships only develop as we spend time with another person, so our intimate relationship with God depends on our meeting Him one-on-one. During meditation, we can hear Him speak through His Word and talk with Him through prayer. I like to pray aloud sometimes and to use "flash" prayers during the day.

Put love into action with others. When we look around at what creative Christians accomplish, we usually see many inspiring stories of love in action. Small acts mean much—a note, a check-up phone call, a visit, a gift of food. Many are able to give volunteer service in the community. Others provide monetary support for worthwhile causes. The Lord leads each of us to give of talents and resources in different ways, enriching us all.

✧

My Prayer

Father, help me spend quality quiet time with You,
that Your love may envelop me and spill over to others. Amen.

My Goal

To live so that Christ's love fills me and reaches others.

My Commitment This Week

Choose two or more activities:

___ Thank God daily for loving me so much that He gave His Son to die for my salvation.

___ Spend at least ten minutes each day in Scripture reading and prayer, with a goal of increasing that time.

___ Ask God to help me reach out to a lonely person.

___ Write a paraphrase of Psalm 15, expressing to God the character I want to develop.

___ Read the thirteenth chapter of 1 Corinthians daily, using different translations.

28. Sins of the Saints

Read 1 John 1:5–10

If we say that we have no sin, we deceive ourselves,
and the truth is not in us.
1 John 1:8

A minister delivered a disturbing sermon on sin, using vivid examples. At the close of the service, an elderly woman approached him, obviously disturbed. "But surely," she said, "*our* sins are not the same as those."

"You're right," he agreed. "Ours are worse!"

We don't know the specific sins the preacher and parishioner were referring to. We do know God is displeased with any sin—the incredible atrocities we learn about daily through TV, newspapers, and other media, *and* those "everyday" transgressions in our own lives that we too readily excuse. Yet doesn't the minister have a valid point? Aren't the sins of believers doubly deplorable? First, because we know better. Second, because our sins send a wrong message about the depth of our faith.

Unger's Bible Dictionary describes sin as "everything in the disposition and purpose and conduct of God's moral creatures that is contrary to the expressed will of God." Checking the Bible, we find God's will about His desired behavior for believers clearly expressed. Moreover, He gives us a role model, His Son, the only sinless person who ever lived. When we examine our lives today in the light of His life, most of us find areas needing improvement. A few check-up questions:

Do I judge others? Jesus said, "Judge not, that you be not judged . . . . And why do you look at the speck in your brother's eye, but do not consider the plank in your own eye?" (Matt. 7:1, 3).

Do I complain? James admonished, "Do not grumble against one another, brethren, lest you be condemned" (James 5:9).

Am I fearful? Paul told Timothy, "God has not given us a spirit of fear, but of power and of love" (2 Tim. 1:7).

Do I readily forgive? Jesus said, "If you forgive men their trespasses, your heavenly Father will also forgive you" (Matt. 6:14).

Do I make hurtful remarks? James called the tongue "an unruly evil, full of deadly poison" (James 3:8). The psalmist tells us, "Keep your tongue from evil, and your lips from speaking guile" (Ps. 34:13).

Do I put my faith into action? Do I use my gifts, show kindness, pray for others? James said, "Faith by itself, if it does not have works, is dead" (James 2:17).

As I review these questions, I give thanks for the in-dwelling Spirit, without whose power my sinful nature would rule my life.

My Prayer

Father, this week, keep me aware of subtle sins and strengthen my ability to lead a more righteous life. Amen.

My Goal

To live under God's power so that I keep my sins to a minimum.

My Commitment This Week

Choose two or more activities:

___ Thank God that He forgives my sins when I confess them.

___ Apply the six check-up questions in this meditation each day. Ask God's forgiveness when I fail and for His help in improving.

___ Ask God to alert me to subtle sins that I overlook.

___ Ask God to guide me in reaching out to someone who holds a grudge against me or another person.

___ Read the short, practical Book of James, one chapter each day, asking God to help me connect it to my life.

✧

29. Let Go and Let God

Read 1 Peter 5:6–11

*Humble yourselves
under the mighty hand of God . . . casting all your care on
Him, for He cares for you.*
1 Peter 5:6–7

A man encased in a body cast for twenty-five months following an automobile accident (due to another driver's negligence) validated the slogan "Let Go and Let God" for me. I met him toward the end of his recovery period. Then sixty-three, he told me about handling the pain from his injuries and of dealing with the divorce from his wife of thirty-two years. I asked how he managed it.

"A five letter word spelled B-I-B-L-E," he said. "I spent most of my waking hours reading the Bible and meditating. I wish I could convince people that the answers to their problems are all there in that book."

He told of regaining consciousness in an examining room where three surgeons concurred that both legs must be amputated. "It was my lowest moment. I closed my eyes and began to pray. Then a fourth surgeon, a young woman, said she could patch me up. I turned my case over to her."

"Were your legs the main problem?" I asked.

"Both hips were crushed, my left arm and many ribs were broken, and more internal injuries than I can name."

His new doctor cautioned him that she could save his legs, but that he probably would never walk on them. "You just save them," I told her. "My Great Physician and I will manage the walking."

About ninety-six hours after the patient was wheeled into surgery, he awakened in a body cast that covered all but his head, right arm, and part of his right foot. While still in the cast, his emotional pain was exacerbated by a surprise visit from two young men carrying brief cases. They served him with divorce papers. "My wife couldn't take being married to an invalid. I was sorry, but all I could do was turn it over to God and my lawyer."

"But how did you keep from becoming bitter?"

"The Bible calls enmity sinful. And with all I had wrong, I didn't need to add ulcers. That's what bitterness brings."

A few weeks later, another surprise visitor appeared, the judge handling the divorce. "He told me that since I couldn't come to him, the only equitable thing was for him to visit me." When the settlement was explained, I thought I saw God's guidance for the judge.

Releasing our troubles to God remains difficult. Too often we hand them over and then snatch them back. But as we learn more about casting all our cares on Him and *leaving* them, we will sense His peace—as did the man in the cast who eventually walked with a cane.

✧

My Prayer

Father, teach me how to let go and release
unsolvable problems into Your all-powerful hands. Amen.

My Goal

To learn to depend on God for my unsolvable problems.

My Commitment This Week

Choose two or more activities:

___ Thank God that He accepts all my problems—large and small.

___ Write, "Lord, what am I to do about . . . ?" Put the paper away. Check each week until I know the answer.

___ Pray for someone with a problem. Tell the person.

___ Use the hymn "I Surrender All" as my prayer.

___ Ask God to impress on my mind a person who might find encouragement from the example in this meditation.

✧

30. The Source of Joy

Read Acts 16:22–34

*When they saw the star, they rejoiced with
exceedingly great joy.*
Matthew 2:10

The euphoria exhibited by the wise men when they
sighted the star two thousand years ago set exactly the
right tone. They realized they would soon meet the Person destined to dispense a supernatural joy reserved for
those who claim Christ as Savior.

If asked to define *joy*, most of us would probably
mention "happiness." But the two feelings differ, especially the soul-joy that Christ brings.

Consider the incredible incident recorded in Acts 16,
when Paul and Silas languished in prison with their feet
in stocks. They couldn't be described as happy. Yet at
midnight they were singing praises to God with such joy
that He caused an earthquake to free them. Their behavior and refusal to escape so impressed the jailer that he
and his household became believers.

C. S. Lewis, the popular British theologian who
gained a wide following in the United States, experienced such joy. It became the focus of the book *Surprised
by Joy*, detailing how he passed from atheism to Christianity. He said the account might appeal especially to
those apt to respond, as others already had when he men-
tioned the sensation: "What! Have you felt it too? I
thought I was the only one."

Joy is outlined in Galatians as one of the nine spiritual gifts to believers. Further, Jesus named spiritual joy
as a permanent gift. He promised, "Your joy no one will
take from you" (John 16:22).

How do we say "thank you" for this precious gift? A
good first step: tell God we want to become one link in

the chain that helps lead others to the source of everlasting joy. He knows all about us and will direct us down different paths, according to our talents and another person's need. For instance, He used many people to draw me into a deeper faith. Three examples stand out in my mind:

The joy bubbling forth from a radiant Christian in her forties suffering from terminal cancer literally "infected" me. I yearned for the depth of faith she projected.

The sensible suggestions provided by several people as I sought to grasp the mysteries of the Bible and learn to read it with more understanding and personal application.

The success stories shared by Christians whom God had guided through difficult situations and smaller "everyday" problems. I began to trust Him for answers.

I soon learned from experience that the steps taken toward a deeper faith produce a deeper joy and serenity.

✧

My Prayer

Father, thank You for showing me the source of joy. Use me to help others find it as I grow in faith. Amen.

My Goal

To share my Christian joy with others.

My Commitment This Week

Choose two or more activities:

___ Thank God for the joy of belonging to His family.

___ Ask God for guidance and power to grow in faith so my joy is pleasing to Him and evident to others.

___ Ask God to show me someone whom I can tell what God has done for me.

___ Read Philippians 4:4–9. List directives and promises of God.

___ Challenge a friend to try the exercise just prior to this one and talk about our findings over coffee.

31. Looking for God

Read Hebrews 11:1–7

He who comes to God must believe that He is, and that He is a rewarder of those who diligently seek Him.
Hebrews 11:6

Diligently seeking to know God better constitutes a rewarding lifetime adventure, claims Paul Tournier, a Swiss psychiatrist and author of *The Adventure of Living*.

Dr. Tournier wrote of observations in treating patients over many decades. "There is a need for fulfillment that is part of the stuff of life itself . . . a thirst for the absolute, which in the last analysis is an expression of man's hunger and thirst after God." He said true happiness will elude us until we recognize that only through holiness and a deeper knowledge of God can we find fulfillment.

God reveals Himself to us through many paths—such as daily Bible study, prayer, meditation, inspired Christian books, friends, and worship services. We see Him in the colors of a sunrise. We hear Him speaking to us through "a still small voice" at times, often related to a problem put before Him. Sometimes He simply impresses on our minds something He wants us to do.

I once queried Deanna, a woman I'd heard practiced a method of looking for God in everyday events. When asked to tell me about it, her face radiated excitement.

"I want to know God better," she said. "I ask Him to reveal something daily, completely orchestrated by His hand. I also ask for sensitivity to recognize what attribute of God is illustrated by the incident." She jots down brief notes on her calendar, including what she learned about God. She says the exercise keeps her looking for Him and seeing Him at work. Here are two of many examples she shared.

Her married daughter suffered a severe case of chicken pox, causing the family great concern. A year later, fully recovered, she called to report her pregnancy and that she expected twins. Deanna's calendar entry about the situation noted the mercy and grace of God in not allowing the pregnancy until complete healing from the contagious viral disease had taken place.

A disturbing encounter occurred in the grocery store where Deanna was shopping for a group of senior adults. Irritated by a comment of an acquaintance, she responded in kind. On returning to her car, she inserted a tape a friend wanted her to hear. She thought it would erase the incident from her mind. What she heard produced the opposite effect. "Our lesson is based on Ephesians 4:29, 'Do not let any unwholesome talk come out of your mouths'" (NIV). God gave her an apt illustration of His love. "Whom the Lord loves He chastens" (Heb. 12:6).

✧

My Prayer

Father, help me know You better by seeing Your hand everywhere, including the ordinary events of daily life. Amen.

My Goal

To embark on a daily adventure to know God better.

My Commitment This Week

Choose two or more activities:

___ Thank God that He will respond when I diligently seek Him.

___ Meditate on Psalm 19. Copy and memorize verse 14.

___ Search for attributes of God in daily Bible reading and everyday events and write them down.

___ Ask God to help me hear and respond to His "still small voice."

___ Read *Experiencing God* by Henry T. Blackaby and Claude V. King.

32. The Heavenly Shepherd

Read Psalm 23

The Lord is my shepherd.
Psalm 23:1

My sister Norma reported acute discomfort during her first attempt at an MRI procedure ordered by the doctor to aid in diagnosis. "I was in a state of panic," she said. "I had to come out of that claustrophobic cavern. The second try, I closed my eyes and began repeating the Twenty-third Psalm. A calmness enveloped me and I made it just fine."

This beloved psalm probably garners more attention than any other Bible portion except the Lord's Prayer. We sing it. My sister memorized it as a child and was still reciting it at age sixty-six. It brings peace to the dying and comfort to the bereaved. What accounts for the popularity of this psalm by David, the shepherd king? Perhaps we revel in the reminder of God's care for His individual sheep.

The Lord is my shepherd. Most of us lack a full understanding of the deep, intimate link between a shepherd and each of his sheep. Yet we sense it when Jesus said, "I am the Good Shepherd." He was announcing His intent to guide and protect those in His flock.

Phillip Keller, author of the classic, *A Shepherd Looks at Psalm 23*, said, "Sheep require, more than any other class of livestock, endless attention and meticulous care." He saw many parallels between sheep and humans, such as fearfulness, stubbornness, and timidity. Yet our heavenly Shepherd delights in caring for us.

I shall not want. Affirming complete trust in our heavenly Caregiver banishes fear. We may not get everything we desire, but He will provide for our needs. We will face tribulations; yet yielding to the Good Shepherd's management, we find peace and contentment.

He makes me to lie down in green pastures. Dry, rocky land comprised David's Palestine. Even with the provision of scarce patches of green pasture, Keller said sheep will not lie down if they are fearful, tormented by pests, hungry, or aggravated by other sheep. As with people, a disturbed flock does not do well. Yet the skilled shepherd takes care of pests and provides fields for grazing. His very presence helps quell fear and rivalry.

He leads me beside the still waters. The shepherd guides his sheep to the best source of water. Also, "still water" comes from dew clinging to the leaves and grass, which sheep feed on just before dawn or during bright moonlight. Similarly, many Christians find that morning meditations satisfy their spiritual thirst, invigorating them for the day ahead.

✧

My Prayer

Father, thank You that You are my Shepherd. Help me to be an ever-more-obedient part of Your flock. Amen.

My Goal

To grasp the full meaning of the Lord as my Shepherd.

My Commitment This Week

Choose two or more activities:

___ Give thanks to God that He is my Shepherd and ask Him to help me learn to follow Him more closely.

___ Read Psalm 23 each day, in different translations.

___ Read (or re-read) the book *A Shepherd Looks at Psalm 23* by Phillip Keller.

___ Use the hymn "Savior, Like a Shepherd Lead Us" as a prayer, substituting "I" and "me" for "we" and "us."

___ Read and discuss Psalm 23 with a shut-in.

33. The Scapegoat

Read Leviticus 16:5–10, 21–22

The scapegoat shall be presented alive before the LORD to be used for making atonement. . . . The goat will carry on itself all their sins to a solitary place.
Leviticus 16:10,22, NIV

"I don't know why I got into some of the things I did when I was young," confided a friend. "I still feel guilty after all these years."

"I know what you mean," I said, thinking about events in my life many decades earlier. "But once we confess and receive God's forgiveness, don't you think He erases them?"

The roots of God's plan for forgiveness go back to Old Testament times when He was forging a new nation of His chosen people. He spoke to Christians across the centuries through a pair of unique sacrifices He prescribed through Moses.

As priest, Aaron followed instructions to take two goats from the people on the annual Day of Atonement. The first goat was sacrificed as an offering to God for the sins of the Israelites. On the head of the second, named the scapegoat, Aaron symbolically placed the nation's sins. He then sent it into the desert to die. Thus the penalty for sin was paid, and the sins and guilt associated with them promptly disappeared.

Moving ahead to New Testament times, consider the first Good Friday. Contemplate afresh how God replaced the two yearly animal sacrifices with the blood of His beloved, sinless Son. Christ paid the penalty once and for all time, becoming a willing scapegoat to carry the sin and guilt of believers into oblivion. At the cross, God clearly demonstrated both His abhorrence of sin and His unlimited love.

How do we respond with our own love to this awesome act on our behalf? A good answer comes from the apostle John, who echoed an admonition repeated throughout the Old and New Testaments. "This is love: that we walk in obedience to his commands" (2 John 6, NIV). Many of us try to keep tuned in to God's commands by recharging our spiritual batteries during Sunday worship. Yet even when we follow up with Bible study and prayer, we find ourselves breaking those commands.

Our sinful nature strives to lead us away from obedience—in subtle ways. Unless we call daily on help from the Holy Spirit, we discover an unkind word slipping out, an unforgiving thought lodging in our mind, a good deed going undone. Thankfully, God's love arrives new every morning. We know His power linked to a willing heart can transform our daily lives.

✧

My Prayer

Father, in wonder and awe I thank You for the sacrifice made at the cross. Give me an obedient heart so that my life reflects my love for You. Amen.

My Goal

To follow God's commandments, living a life that honors Him and reflects my gratitude to Him.

My Commitment This Week

Choose two or more activities:

___ Give thanks that Christ became a scapegoat on my behalf, carrying my confessed sins into oblivion.

___ Ask God to alert me to habits that are at odds with His commands. Confess sins, asking His forgiveness.

___ Meditate on Psalm 51. Memorize verses 10–11.

___ Pray the words of the hymn "Rock of Ages."

___ Forgive and pray for someone who has hurt me through an unkind word or action.

34. Heart-Cleaning Time

Read Matthew 12:33–37

For out of the abundance of the heart the mouth speaks.
Matthew 12:34

Our houses periodically need a thorough cleaning. An exchange I saw on a TV program prompted me to believe we sometimes need meticulous heart-cleaning as well.

A man told of traveling on a New York subway when a father with several children boarded. The children began misbehaving and the father did nothing to stop them. When a nearby passenger suggested he quiet them, the father said, "I guess I should but we just buried their mother. They don't know how to handle it, and I guess I don't either."

Having lived in New York City for many years just prior to retirement, I easily envisioned myself on that subway. At the very least, I knew I would have mentally judged the father for his failure to act. Also, I probably would have complained to fellow travelers. The Bible says both responses are sinful. In the Sermon on the Mount, Jesus told His disciples He wanted them to shine as lights of the world, not act as its judges.

The subway story produced a positive as well as a disturbing effect. It helped me focus on the need to clean out all wrong attitudes and unhealthy habits, such as the tendency to rush to judgment without knowing the facts. The beginning of a new week presents a good opportunity to search the heart, asking for God's help in removing unwanted habits. The apostle Paul reminded the Christians at Ephesus, "Let no corrupt communication proceed out of your mouth. . . . Let all bitterness, wrath, anger, clamor and evil speaking be put away. . . . Walk as children of light" (Eph. 4:29,31; 5:8).

How do we walk as children of light? Jesus said we can never do it on our own. Yet as we abide in Him and remain obedient to His leading, He will transform us into the people He wants us to be. He will help us replace wrong thoughts, words, and actions with His gifts of the Spirit. Paul names them: "love, joy, peace, long-suffering, kindness, goodness, faithfulness, gentleness, self-control" (Gal. 5:22–23).

A good theme verse for this week: "Let your light so shine before men, that they may see your good works and glorify your Father in heaven" (Matt. 5:16). God wants us to serve as His ambassadors of light and will honor prayers asking for help. Yet we need His help daily because wrong habits will work hard to take control.

✧

My Prayer

*Father, today and every day, fill me afresh with Your
Holy Spirit, so that what I think, say,
and do will be controlled by You;
and Your name will be glorified. Amen.*

My Goal

To cleanse my heart and mind from unhealthy attitudes so that what comes from my mouth is pleasing to God.

My Commitment This Week

Choose two or more activities:

___ Review Paul's reminders in today's meditation in light of my own behavior and decide which areas I need to correct.

___ Study the nine gifts of the Spirit outlined in Galatians and ask God to help me activate them.

___ Meditate on Matthew 5:13–16. Copy and memorize verse 16. Make it my "verse for the week."

___ Ask God to help me love someone I judged.

___ Make a list of practical ways I can let God's light shine through me to others.

✧

35. Choices

Read Luke 10:38–42

*But one thing is needed, and Mary has chosen that good part,
which will not be taken away from her.*
Luke 10:42

When actress Jessica Tandy died in 1994 at age eighty-five, *Time* magazine described her as "a gracious star at ease with age." The memorable roles she chose to continue creating in her seventies and early eighties provided ample proof of *Time's* assessment.

Ms. Tandy earned the "Best Actress" Oscar in 1990 for the movie, *Driving Miss Daisy.* In June 1994, she stepped on stage for the last time, with husband Hume Cronyn, to accept the Tony award for "Lifetime Achievement." She chose to make this final appearance in spite of her debilitating five-year battle with cancer. In doing so, she treated her rapt audience to a lasting image of elegance and dignity rising above physical distress.

Jesus taught a valuable lesson about choices when He visited in the home of Martha and Mary. Both sisters wanted to make Jesus feel welcome. Yet Martha became distracted with her many duties while Mary sat at Jesus' feet, listening eagerly to His teaching. When Martha chided Jesus for not telling Mary to do her share of the work, Jesus gently rebuked Martha. He told her Mary had made the better choice. He said, in essence, that "In your relationship to Me, you must not only give but take time to receive."

The message of Joshua, who assumed leadership of the children of Israel when Moses died, challenges us as it did God's chosen people when he led them to the promised land. He told them to "choose for yourselves this day whom you will serve. . . . But as for me and my house, we will serve the LORD" (Josh. 24:15).

Pondering these biblical directives, I realize afresh the graciousness of God in providing His indwelling Spirit to help believers make right choices. Yet we must seek His guidance, whether a major issue looms or one of less consequence. Some examples:

✧ Will I choose to greet each day with a happy outlook, thanking God for my blessings, or dwell on my aches and pains?

✧ Will I choose to turn a deep concern over to God in complete trust, or continue fretting about it?

✧ Will I choose to take time for daily Bible study and prayer, or rely on "third-party" teaching?

✧ Will I choose to commit each day and its activities to His direction, or "go it alone"?

✧ Will I choose to pursue my own agenda, or pause to visit a friend who is lonely?

The many choices we make daily help shape the person the world sees now and the legacy we leave.

✧

My Prayer

Father, thank You for the freedom to make choices, and for Your indwelling Spirit to help me make right ones. Amen.

My Goal

To seek the Lord's guidance in making choices.

My Commitment This Week

Choose two or more activities:

___ On awakening each morning, offer praises to God for the day ahead and thank Him for His guidance.

___ Read Joshua 24:13–16 and write down *my* choice about God.

___ Choose to make time for daily Bible study and prayer.

___ List the pros and cons of situations about which I must make a choice and seek God's guidance.

___ Read and share *The Christian's Secret of a Happy Life* by Hannah Whitall Smith.

36. Useful at Eighty

Read Exodus 3:1–12

God called to him from the midst of the bush and said, "Moses, Moses!" And he said, "Here I am."
Exodus 3:4

"I'm excited to be studying the life of Moses," said an exuberant grandmother as our Bible group reached the "burning bush" chapter in Exodus. We nodded in agreement as she elaborated.

"He was eighty years old!" she exclaimed. "I find that very encouraging. Maybe the Lord can still use me."

When Moses received the call to serve as God's man to liberate His chosen people, he exhibited no enthusiasm for the honor. He felt totally inadequate. "Why me?" he asked God. After all, he'd spent the last forty years tending sheep for his father-in-law, hardly the credentials needed for such an assignment. He claimed that: (1) the Hebrews wouldn't accept him as a leader; (2) Pharaoh wouldn't pay any attention to him; and (3) he was a poor speaker. Further, he said nobody would believe he spoke for God.

God listened to Moses but did not change His mind. However, He did make the all-important promise essential to the mission's success. Put simply, He said, "I will be with you. I'll tell you exactly what to do and what to say." He also said that Moses' eloquent brother, Aaron, could be his mouthpiece, delivering the words the Lord gave Moses. God even sketched out His master plan to free the Israelites from Egyptian captivity.

Looking back at Moses' call and the beginning stages of his forty-year assignment, we see some of the character traits that make a woman or man useful to God.

Humility. Moses was not a weak man, but he recognized his inadequacies and God's limitless strengths. He realized that without God he could do nothing. Linked to God and His plan, anything was possible.

Faith. From the time of the burning bush, Moses kept his eyes on God. He believed God was who He claimed to be and that He could be trusted. He talked to Him constantly, seeking guidance.

Obedience. Moses possessed a willing spirit, eager to be taught. Once he accepted God's claim on him, he listened and did as He commanded even though it appeared futile at times.

Courage. Moses stood before Pharaoh, the most powerful monarch of his day, and delivered God's message. Moses could carry out this awesome task because he feared and trusted God.

God will help us develop the same character traits that Moses exhibited. We need only approach Him with a willing spirit, in complete trust and obedience.

My Prayer

Father, mold me as You molded Moses, so that I may fulfill the role You have for me in building Your kingdom on earth.
Amen.

My Goal

To develop the same character traits as Moses.

My Commitment This Week

Choose two or more activities:

___ Give thanks for the lessons from the Bible that illustrate the character traits God wants in me.

___ Daily review the character traits in Moses that made him useful to God. Ask Him to help me develop them.

___ Ask God to guide me to any work He wants me to do and strengthen me to do it willingly and well.

___ Make a page in my notebook for each word—*humility, faith, obedience, courage*—and copy meaningful Bible verses.

___ Read *Moses: Freeing Yourself to Know God* in the *Men of Character* series by Gene Getz (Broadman & Holman, 1996).

37. Is It His Voice?

Read Psalm 121

For this is God . . . He will be our guide even to death.
Psalm 48:14

"Have you made a decision?" I asked my friend, whose eighty-five-year-old mother was considering surgery.

"Yes," she said, with obvious relief. "We're not going to have the surgery." She and her mother had sought a second opinion. It opposed that of the first physician.

"You seem to have peace about it," I said.

"Oh, I do. I do. The specialist recommended against it and spelled out his reasons." She told me about them.

A number of us prayed for several days seeking God's wisdom for those involved in the decision and for a sense of peace following the resolution. She said she knew the prayers helped.

When we want God's guidance on a specific matter—whether something major or small—we are promised He will respond. But *how*? Christians who seek help find that He speaks through at least four channels.

Through Scripture. God will never direct us down a path contrary to principles for daily living as outlined in the Bible.

A Christian friend experiencing a painful divorce became angry at her daughter, who insisted on remaining friends with her father. The mother fired off a letter to her daughter, producing a rift that never healed. Yet God spoke plainly in the Bible about our need to forgive.

Through judgment and common sense. God's voice may reach us through the faculties given us or through trusted friends. I also find I need guidance in exercising judgment. When facing a driving test, I consulted a relative who had taught driving. Then I asked God to help me study the training manual with understanding and to retain what I learned. (God wouldn't help me pass a test I hadn't prepared for!)

Through inward impressions. When about to undertake something God doesn't want us to do (even though a worthy thing), we will feel unsettled and confused. We must wait. When we proceed in His will, we will experience a wonderful peace, as my friend did with the decision about her mother's surgery.

Through providential circumstance. If an inner impression about an action comes from God, He will open a door for it. In the parable of the good Shepherd, Jesus proclaimed Himself the door of the sheep. "My sheep hear My voice, and I know them, and they follow Me" (John 10:27). He opens the way; we follow.

Whenever I pose a dilemma to God in fervent prayer, He faithfully guides, not always as swiftly as I might like, but on His perfect timetable.

✧

My Prayer

Father, thank You for Your guidance. Help me remember to ask, and to hear and obey Your voice. Amen.

My Goal

To learn to discern God's will.

My Commitment This Week

Choose two or more activities:

___ Write down the four reminders in this meditation about how God may guide. Post in a convenient place.

___ Pray about decisions I must make, using the four guidelines.

___ Explore personal experiences with a Christian friend who has faced difficult decisions. Share these guidelines.

___ Pray Psalm 143:7–12. Make verse 10 my verse for the week.

___ Write a letter to an out-of-town friend, including a report of a personal experience telling them how God guided.

38. A New Calling

Read Matthew 25:14–30

You have been faithful with a few things; I will put you in charge of many things.
Matthew 25:21, NIV

"We didn't want to retire *from* teaching as much as to re-tire *to* something else," explained my sister Norma about the commitment she and her husband made to hospice and other volunteer work.

"During our last year in the classroom, we began asking God what He wanted us to do next," she said. "We looked forward to more time with our grandchildren, RV travel, and fishing; but we felt our lives also needed a

Christian dimension focusing on others. We were healthy and not yet sixty-five."

The Lord led the new retirees into that Christian dimension step by step. As they told of the successive jobs He had given them, I thought of the parable of the talents.

First they agreed to lead a weekly Bible class. The talk there alerted them to the need to visit shut-ins and nursing homes. The next assignment: leadership of a new monthly Sunshine Club for older adults, which grew to eighty or more seniors.

When a Sunshine luncheon speaker explained the local hospice program and the role of volunteers, the couple sensed a nudge to investigate. Soon they enrolled in a training program, and eventually began reaching out to the terminally ill and their caregivers, including a year's follow-up with bereaved families. After five years with Hospice, their minister asked them to assist with a grief recovery program open to anyone in the community who has lost a loved one.

The couple's involvement with seniors led to membership on a denominational committee to help devise an outreach program for older adults, covering the northeastern part of Texas. An RV Rally/Retreat resulted, which was attended by twelve couples. In six years the semi-annual event outgrew its first location and began attracting up to one hundred people from twenty churches.

Norma said her husband Buford took on two other jobs for which she just gave background support. After attending lay leadership training he received certification to speak at small nearby churches. At first he resisted the second job—to lead a Bible study. But when told the request had come from several prisoners, he soon began a Thursday evening ministry at the local jail.

The couple report countless personal blessings from encounters during volunteer work, as do most people who serve others. "We are blessed when those dealing with a traumatic loss simply thank us for listening or praying with them," said Norma. "We are grateful to God for permitting us to be His instruments."

My Prayer

Father, thank You for those who selflessly serve others. Show me how You would have me reach out. Amen.

My Goal

To become responsive to ways God would have me serve.

My Commitment This Week

Choose two or more activities:

___ Ask God to enable me to recognize and follow through with at least one thing I can do to help someone.

___ Think of volunteers I know who are making a difference in people's lives, and give thanks for them.

___ Visit someone who has lost a loved one recently.

___ Investigate local organizations that deal with the terminally ill and consider volunteering.

___ Discover and share information about local support groups with someone who is grieving.

39. The Inheritance

Read 1 Peter 1:3–11

An inheritance incorruptible and undefiled and that does not fade away.
1 Peter 1:4

Once upon a time there was a wealthy young man who seemed to have it all—rewarding career, beautiful mansion complete with swimming pool and tennis court, cars, and a private jet. His beloved wife was expecting their first child. He radiated joy.

His joy was dealt a severe blow by the death of his wife when their son was born. Yet he determined to care for the baby to the best of his ability. He engaged a middle-aged woman to live at the mansion and help raise the boy; no expense was spared. The father proudly watched the boy develop into a fine young man. He was accepted at a top university. Then another blow—a car accident claimed the boy's life in his senior year. The father was devastated. He soon followed his son in death.

The man's lawyer summoned all former employees. He told them the will stipulated that each was to go through the house and choose one thing. One selected a silver coffee service, another a piece of furniture, another a crystal chandelier. The woman who raised the boy reached for a photograph of him on the mantle, assuring the lawyer that this was all she wanted. He removed the photograph from the frame and read the inscription on the back: "The one who chooses my son inherits my wealth."

The truth of this modern parable is apparent to Christians. Yet, too often we fail to claim the "wealth" we've inherited. Some riches the Bible spells out:

Peace. "You will keep him in perfect peace, whose mind is stayed on You" (Isa. 26:3).

Comfort. "Blessed are those who mourn, for they shall be comforted" (Matt. 5:4).

Love. "His love has been perfected in us" (1 John 4:12).

Guidance. "In all your ways acknowledge Him, and He shall direct your paths" (Prov. 3:6).

Strength. "But those who wait on the LORD shall renew their strength" (Isa. 40:31).

Rest. "Come to Me, all you who labor and are heavy laden, and I will give you rest" (Matt. 11:28).

Wisdom. "If any of you lacks wisdom, let him ask of God, who gives to all liberally" (James 1:5).

When we compare these seven intangible gifts with the material goods we accumulate, we begin to recognize what truly shapes the "abundant life" of the Christian.

✧

My Prayer

Father, thank You for the riches You have showered on me. Please help me use my inheritance to the fullest. Amen.

My Goal

To explore my inheritance as a Christian and use it in ways that glorify God.

My Commitment This Week

Choose two or more activities:

___ Thank God for the abundant spiritual inheritance He has given me.

___ List the "spiritual riches" I inherit as a Christian and post it where I can see it frequently.

___ Meditate on one of the seven Scripture verses each day, asking God to help me apply it to my life.

___ With thanksgiving, make the words of the hymn "Great Is Thy Faithfulness" my prayer.

___ Write a letter to a friend, mentioning the "spiritual riches" I find especially meaningful.

✧

40. A Prisoner's Plea

Read Ephesians 4:1–6

Live a life worthy of the calling you have received.
Be completely humble and gentle; be patient,
bearing with one another in love.
Ephesians 4:1–2, NIV

While in prison, probably in Rome, Paul remained impervious to civil authority, focusing instead on his ownership by God. His goal: to fulfill his responsibility as God's messenger.

Most especially, Paul wanted to help believers become more Christlike in their response to God's goodness in choosing them. Three basic elements of Christian character—humility, gentleness, and patience—outlined by Paul in the first century, remain compelling directives today as well.

When I was in my sixties, God used a visit to a nephew and niece thirty years younger to teach me a valuable lesson about developing these character traits. A talkative man from across the street stopped by as my niece was exploring a complicated situation with me. While privy to only a smattering of our conversation, he offered definitive views. Startled by his instant interference, I judged his suggestion worthless; but my niece graciously thanked him. In the next few days, we received more unsolicited pronouncements by the "know-it-all" neighbor, with my niece's same gentle response.

"I'm impressed with your kindness," I said to her. "I'd be tempted to tell him to mind his own business."

"Oh, I'm grateful to God for him," she replied. "I'm a very impatient person, and some time ago I asked God to help me do better. I'm sure He gave me this neighbor to practice on." When we ask God to help correct traits that are not Christlike, He will respond. Sometimes that help is direct. Other times we learn by observing fellow Christians (as I did) or by studying the lives of obedient men and women of the Bible.

Humility and *gentleness* may be mistakenly equated with self-disparagement and weakness. Sometimes Christians "confess" shortcomings so others will say, "Oh no. You're not like that at all." True humility simply means recognizing one is dependent on God, that He is the source of all good, and that credit belongs to Him. Moses exemplified meekness *and* strength as he led a rebellious nation to the promised land. He relied on God's direction daily.

Patience, called "long-suffering" in the King James Version, becomes especially difficult when you believe the other person is wrong. Yet when yielded to the Holy Spirit's control, we will exhibit forbearance in love, leaving the outcome to God.

Without God's help, I know I will fall short in character building. As I follow His leading, I can count on Him to help me grow more like Christ.

✧

My Prayer

Father, this week, please guide my thoughts, words, and actions so my life reflects Christlike qualities. Amen.

My Goal

To live a life that reflects the Christlike qualities of humility, gentleness, and patience.

My Commitment This Week

Choose two or more activities:

___ Thank God that He chose me as part of His family.

___ Give thanks for the Bible and its teaching about the personal qualities God wants us to develop.

___ Ask God to signal me when I fail to exhibit humility, gentleness, and patience as I interact with people.

___ Ask forgiveness when I fail to exhibit Christlike qualities.

___ Read Colossians 3:12–25 to review other desirable characteristics of the Christian and the Christian home.

✧

41. Fear: The Plus Side

Read Mark 4:35–41

But He said to them, "Why are you so fearful?
How is it that you have no faith?"
Mark 4:40

A hill-climbing adventure pursued by a group of tourists became especially exhilarating to one young woman. She reveled in scaling the steep, arduous slope. But on reaching the top and turning to survey her route, her joyous spirit evaporated. Panic enveloped her. She simply couldn't handle the prospect of picking her way back down. Only with the strong assistance of two friends did she manage a slow descent.

The fear that gripped the young climber was not unlike that which claimed Jesus' disciples on one particular occasion. Jesus had been patiently teaching the crowds on shore from His boat-pulpit. In the evening He got in the boat with His disciples and set out for the other side of the lake. Jesus was in the stern asleep, when a violent windstorm arose. With waves beating into the boat, the disciples awoke Him, saying, "Teacher, do You not care that we are perishing?" (Mark 4:38).

Jesus arose and rebuked the wind and the sea. All was calm. Then He chided the disciples for being fearful, asking, "How is it that you have no faith?" (Mark 4:40). Awe swept over them as they realized His power even over nature.

Believers through the centuries have turned to Christ, as the disciples did, to still the storms of life; and they have experienced the peace that envelops them in the midst of troubles. They also have learned that the Lord's promises can be trusted. He said specifically that He would never leave nor forsake His children.

As we get older, a variety of fears lie in wait to try to establish residence in our souls. Will I be a burden to my family? Will I become incapacitated? Will I run out of money? Will I be forgotten? What does the future hold for me?

A devout Christian man in his seventies once said he banished all worry about the future by assuring himself, "God hasn't brought me this far to drop me now!" I find myself borrowing this claim when asked if I'm not worried about some shadowy unknown.

Another believer suggests that reviewing past crises in her life and recalling how the Lord brought her through them, blunts fear, fuels her sense of peace, and deepens her faith.

A good reminder comes from the old hymn "What a Friend We Have in Jesus," as it claims:

> *O what peace we often forfeit,*
> *O what needless pain we bear,*
> *All because we do not carry*
> *Everything to God in prayer!*
>
> ✧

My Prayer

Father, strengthen my faith daily so that I readily release all fears into Your strong, loving hands. Amen.

My Goal

To strengthen my faith so that I will confidently turn any fears over to God.

My Commitment This Week

Choose two or more activities:

___ Thank God daily for His promise that He will never leave me.

___ Review past crises in my life and the lives of loved ones, thanking God for His strengthening hand.

___ Help reassure others when I sense they are fearful.

___ Meditate with gratitude and confidence on the truth of the declarations in the hymn "What a Friend We Have in Jesus."

___ Read Deuteronomy 31:1–8 for the antidote to fear given to Joshua when he was to lead the Israelites.

42. The Inner Voice

Read Acts 8:26–40

Then the Spirit said to Philip, "Go. . . . "
Acts 8:29

"The drive from Dallas to Haskell takes three hours and an ice storm was in the forecast," my nephew Conner told me. "But I couldn't shake the feeling that I needed to go to see my grandmother that Saturday."

He said he remembered the incident vividly, though it occurred ten years earlier. His wife could not accompany him but encouraged him to go, although she was concerned about the weather. He left about noon and found his eighty-nine-year-old grandmother in great spirits.

"I'll bet she was thrilled to see you," I said. The eldest of her six grandchildren, I knew he rated a special place in her heart as well as that of his deceased grandfather, whose name he bears.

"She did seem pleased," he agreed. "We enjoyed dinner and a real good visit. As it turned out, I was the last one in the family to get to visit with her." On the following Monday, she suffered a stroke and could no longer communicate with anyone.

Conner's story illustrates two great truths. First, a loving, merciful God gave Mrs. Conner a special evening alone with her grandson. And He gave *him* a last treasured memory of her. Second, the incident shows the need to stay sensitive to the inner voice directing us to take some action (or sometimes directing us *away* from it).

Such strong impulses virtually always come to the Christian from the Holy Spirit, I believe. Not that outside influences aren't sometimes at work, maybe giving a wrong signal. When in doubt, I ask God to stop me if I have misunderstood. Yet the Bible gives evidence of the validity of that inner voice. One clear example involved a message to Philip, telling him to go to a certain road where he met an Ethiopian official. The apostle subsequently helped the official with Scripture, explained salvation, and baptized a new convert.

Friends tell me about similar experiences when an inner voice tells them to phone, write, or visit someone or to volunteer for some task. As my nephew found, they feel "unsettled" until they comply. When obedient, they discover, as he did, a serendipity in the form of unexpected joys from a simple act. One of these joys surfaces with the realization that one has been an instrument of the Holy Spirit.

❖

My Prayer

Father, keep me responsive to the inner voice
by which You guide. Amen.

My Goal

To be obedient to the inner voice of the Holy Spirit.

My Commitment This Week

Choose two or more activities:

___ Ask God to help me grow ever closer to Him so that I hear and obey when He prompts me to take action.

___ Pray each morning that the Lord will direct my conversations during the day, signaling me if I'm about to say something displeasing to Him.

___ Follow through with any "inner prompting" by first asking the Lord to block the action if the move is wrong.

___ Think about incidents in my life when I felt led to take some action. Exchange stories of such experiences with another Christian.

___ Transform the hymn "Trust and Obey" into my prayer.

43. Faith's Payoff

Read 2 Corinthians 1:3–7

Blessed be the God and Father of our Lord Jesus Christ, the Father of mercies and God of all comfort.
2 Corinthians 1:3

"This was a time in my life when a mature faith paid off," said Gifford Long, a young minister. He referred to a crisis he faced and what he learned from it about the comfort of knowing Jesus.

He had taken his wife, expecting twins, to the doctor for a routine check-up. During the visit, the doctor discovered that one twin had died in the womb.

While rushing to the hospital and then waiting for the emergency C-section, fear gripped Gifford. He experienced the sensation of sinking. "I didn't know whether my wife or second daughter would survive," he said. "I screamed inside, 'God, help me!'" A calmness enveloped him, followed by an image of Peter walking on the water and sinking. He sensed Jesus pulling him out of the water of despair that had washed over him.

As he sat on the bench outside the nursery, the words of a favorite old Charles Wesley hymn filled his heart:

> *Jesus, Lover of my soul,*
> *Let me to Thy bosom fly,*
> *While the nearer waters roll,*
> *While the tempest still is high:*
> *Hide me, O my Savior, hide,*
> *Till the storm of life is past;*
> *Safe into the haven guide;*
> *O receive my soul at last!*

Pondering Gifford's experience, I marveled at his mature faith while still young. His story serves as a reminder for us at any age—of how to be prepared to handle the inevitable crises that invade our lives.

Strive for a deeper personal relationship with Christ. While many things help us know Christ better, none is more effective than a daily quiet time, when we read the Bible and talk and listen to Him through prayer. Because Gifford knew Christ, he immediately sensed His presence when fear tried to envelop him.

Saturate your mind with Scripture. Backing up quiet time with worship and Bible study enhances the process. Bible verses committed to memory usually surface when needed to comfort and guide. The dairy industry once applied a slogan to physical health: "You never outgrow your need for milk." A related one applies to spiritual health: "You never outgrow your need for God's word."

Call on God when a crisis looms. The cry for help becomes automatic when one is accustomed to daily prayer. God heard and acted on Gifford's brief plea just as He acted on that of Peter two thousand years earlier. Comfort can also come from a prayer circle or Christian friends to call on for prayer support.

The more our faith continues to mature, the more assured we are of God's comfort when the storms of life strike us.

✧

My Prayer

Father, help me become more diligent in working toward a mature faith. Amen.

My Goal

To continue to grow in faith as long as I live.

My Commitment This Week

Choose two or more activities:

___ Thank God for my faith and for helping it grow.

___ Thank God for His comfort when troubles come.

___ Listen to tapes of Scripture when driving, ironing, or doing compatible household tasks.

___ Meditate on the hymn "My Faith Looks Up to Thee."

___ Pray for God to put a desire for a deep faith within the hearts of the young people in my family.

✧

44. The First Step

Read 2 Kings 5:9–16

So he [Naaman] went down and dipped seven times in the Jordan, according to the saying of the man of God; and his flesh was restored.
2 Kings 5:14

Naaman, a valiant army commander suffering from leprosy, was told that a prophet of God in Israel could cure him. He journeyed to the prophet's home, expecting to be cured by a magic wave of the prophet's hand. He left in a rage when the prophet did not even come outside, but sent a message telling Naaman to go wash seven times in the Jordan. His servants finally persuaded him to obey. When he took the step God had commanded, Naaman was healed.

Bob Conger, a retired school superintendent, told of taking a crucial first step prompted by God and being delivered from an unhealthy habit that had held him captive for over twenty-five years. He had been a heavy smoker.

"Whether it was a cigar, a pipe, or a cigarette," he said, "I inhaled deeply, with every drag. At one point I began using a cigarette holder so I could smoke them down to the last eighth of an inch. I didn't throw away a third as some people do."

Through the years, Bob's family and friends would ask him when he was going to stop smoking. His reply was always the same: "Never! I'm not going to quit something I find so enjoyable."

Then Bob and his wife went to a weekend spiritual retreat. During a program break, he stood outside smoking and chatting with friends. One of them repeated the question he'd heard so often and he gave her his usual answer, adding, "So quit bugging me."

He decided to skip the next session and take a hike up a nearby hill. When almost at the top, he suddenly stopped, as the realization hit him that cigarettes had become his master. His prayer was short and specific: "God, I'm going to quit smoking but You'll have to help me." Then he threw his pack of cigarettes and his expensive lighter as far as he could.

"I took the first step," said Bob, "then God took over. What happened next had to be supernatural. I had no withdrawal symptoms and no desire to smoke again."

Over the years I have had friends who struggled to stop smoking or to quit another addictive habit, often unsuccessfully. So I had no difficulty recognizing that supernatural power lay at the heart of Bob's success.

As Bob and I discussed the miraculous way God had delivered him, I asked if he thought the same principle holds for any unhealthy habit. "Yes, I'm sure it does," he said. "But remember, you must take the first step."

✧

My Prayer

Father, thank You for Your power available to help correct weaknesses in my life. Amen.

My Goal

To rid myself of unhealthy habits that detract from the person God wants me to be.

My Commitment This Week

Choose two or more activities:

___ Thank God for the power He provides to help me stop unhealthy habits.

___ Ask God to help me recognize and commit to correcting any habit that needs changing. Record progress in my notebook.

___ Ask God for persistence in making needed changes.

___ Pray for a relative or friend addicted to an unhealthy habit—that God will help the person take the first step.

___ Investigate local support groups that might help me or a friend with a specific problem area.

45. Trust Amid Trials

Read Romans 12:9–18

Be joyful in hope, patient in affliction, faithful in prayer.
Romans 12:12, NIV

Her sparkling eyes and radiant smile of welcome so captivated me that I failed to apologize for my thoughtlessness. I realized too late that I should have phoned before delivering a loaf of "birthday bread" to my neighbor. Physical disabilities largely confined her to home.

When she didn't respond to my ring for a long time, I concluded she was resting, asleep, or simply didn't feel up to entertaining a visitor. But as I turned away, she opened the door and graciously invited me in. When I hesitated, she insisted, "Please come in. You must see my birthday flowers."

As she slowly inched her way down the hall toward the living room, I noted a bandage on one foot. "I feel *so* fortunate to still be able to cook for myself," she said, stopping in the kitchen to check a burner. My neighbor's spirit matched the beauty of the exquisite red roses.

"Each problem, each health setback has just drawn me closer to God," she said. "When I look back, I realize how good He has been to me. He has provided for every need." I told her that her joyous attitude in such adversity was an inspiration. "I don't know how people manage without faith," she said. "Mine hasn't always been as strong as it is now. I'm so thankful."

The next morning, when I flipped over a new page on a desktop Scripture tray, Romans 12:12 beautifully summarized the message from my late afternoon encounter. I read three brief but powerful directives on the card, gently confirming God's lesson to me in writing.

Be joyful in hope, such joy comes in part by Christ's past actions in our lives. Looking back as my friend did fuels hope in the future. We can trust Him. Christ remains the same yesterday, today, and forever.

Be patient in affliction, knowing that God comes to us in our weakness. He uses suffering to show us the tenderness of His love, the wisdom of His ways.

Be faithful in prayer, for as James reminds us, "The effective, fervent prayer of a righteous man avails much" (James 5:16). The apostle Paul urged, "In everything by prayer and supplication, with thanksgiving, let your requests be made known to God" (Phil. 4:6).

✧

My Prayer

Father, thank You for encounters with other Christians who nourish faith, hope, and trust in You. Amen.

My Goal

To strive for deep faith, hope, and trust during trials.

My Commitment This Week

Choose two or more activities:

___ Thank God for His faithfulness in strengthening me to handle problems when they aren't resolved.

___ Bring to God in prayer any serious situation concerning my own life or the life of a loved one.

___ Think of people who exhibit peace during illness. Tell them that their faith helped strengthen mine.

___ Meditate on Psalm 100 and write down the things it tells me to do.

___ Write a letter of encouragement to someone who is carrying a burden. Include a Scripture that has been meaningful (such as Rom. 12:12).

46. *A Prayer Pattern*

Read Psalm 5

In everything by prayer and supplication,
with thanksgiving, let your requests
be made known to God.
Philippians 4:6

John Calvin, the great figure of the Reformation, made a pronouncement about prayer that remains as sensible to-day as in the sixteenth century. He compared failure to pray with knowing about buried treasure in the yard and being too lazy to dig it up. Because of such apathy, the abundant life God wants for His children remains in the ground for too many people.

The truth of Calvin's declaration came home force-fully to me long after I reached middle age. Happily, the awakening to the spiritual poverty of my "cultural Christianity" sent me to my knees and my Bible in ear-nest. Gradually I realized what Jesus meant when He said, "I have come that they may have life, and that they may have it more abundantly" (John 10:10). I thank God often for the full life He provides in my se-nior years.

My friend Martin Thomas calls prayer, "conversations of the heart with God." A conversation means we're to listen and receive as well as to tell and ask.

Most of the time my heart is so full of gratitude for all God is doing and for the sense of His nearness that the conversation proceeds pretty well (though my asking usually overshadows my listening). But sometimes I experience desert seasons when an invisible wall separates me from God. My mind begins skipping about and fixing itself on random situations. When that happens I find help in using the acronym A.C.T.S. to organize and focus my morning prayers.

Adoration combines deep reverence and praise, not something that God needs to receive, but that we need to give. We need to express our love for Him, our awe for the privilege of coming into His presence. Borrowing the words of a psalm (such as 63, 98, or 100) or a favorite hymn enriches this beginning to prayer.

Confession of shortcomings and failures provides the platform for soliciting God's guidance and power to overcome them. Accepting His forgiveness of sins not only brings relief to a troubled spirit but also reminds us to forgive others as readily.

Thanksgiving becomes spontaneous when we think through God's wondrous provisions, faithfulness, and love. Reciting specific blessings helps shrink the problem areas and keep them in perspective.

Supplications or intercessions for others and myself usually claim the largest part of my time with God. I've been praying about several people for years, but new concerns surface regularly. I find that all situations and problems, large or small, benefit from His counsel.

✧

My Prayer

Father, help me converse with You so that I hear You and so that I pray under the Holy Spirit's guidance. Amen.

My Goal

To become more effective in prayer, even in dry periods.

My Commitment This Week

Choose two or more activities:

___ Organize daily prayers around A.C.T.S.

___ Read the little book *ACTS in Prayer* by E. W. Price Jr., and meditate on a different psalm each day.

___ Ask God to guide me in expanding my prayers of intercession, including people in authority in this country and worldwide.

___ Read John 17, a prayer of Jesus in which He prayed not only for His disciples, but also for believers who were to come after them.

___ Pray for those involved when I hear an ambulance, fire engine, or bad news reports.

47. Jesus Christ: Guest or Resident?

Read Revelation 3:15–22

Behold, I stand at the door and knock. If anyone hears My voice and opens the door, I will come in.
Revelation 3:20

A regal lady of nineteenth-century England, well known as a gracious hostess, was also a devout Christian. She frequently invoked the name of the Lord Jesus in her conversation—to the dismay of some of her friends.

Once one of them asked her who was the most distinguished guest she had ever entertained.

"Her majesty, Queen Victoria," she replied immediately.

"What about Jesus Christ? You're always talking about Him," chided her interrogator. "Why didn't you name Him?"

"Oh, Christ is not a guest," she said. "He lives here!"

Pondering this vignette, I placed myself in the midst of the woman's friends. My faith in God, implanted early, remained steady through the years; but Jesus was another matter. I accepted Him as the Son of God who died to save me. But I didn't truly understand His role, nor did I grapple with the concept for many years. The Holy Spirit mystified me totally.

Through my thirties and forties, I experienced periods when I felt that my Christian life lacked depth and my life as a whole didn't count for much. I responded by taking on more responsibilities in my church and in church-sponsored outreach projects in the midst of a demanding business career. In my early fifties, God illuminated my problem: I was focusing on the church instead of its Head.

My middle-age awakening came in part during visits with my family, during which I saw that many of them, including one high-school-age nephew, had a personal relationship with Christ. At that same time, God brought other Christ-centered people into my life. My initial uneasiness about their familiarity with Him was eventually replaced by a growing desire to know Him as they did.

Now age "seventy-something," I know that my quest to know Christ better will continue the rest of my earthly life. Fortunately, His indwelling Holy Spirit helps me: (1) better understand the Bible and how to apply it to my daily life; (2) pray more effectually; (3) discover and follow God's will for me; and (4) gain grace and strength to handle life's ups and downs.

My memory bank stores happy images of days gone by. None compare however, with the joy and contentment that envelop me since Christ became a permanent resident.

✧

My Prayer

Father, thank You for sending Your Son to die for me and live with me. Keep me obedient to His leading. Amen.

My Goal

To experience Christ, guiding me to a deeper faith.

My Commitment This Week

Choose two or more activities:

___ Thank God that I can call myself a Christian.

___ On awakening, to ask God to fill me afresh with His Spirit to guide my words and actions.

___ Sing or read "I Am Thine, O Lord" as my prayer.

___ List the talents God has given me, and ask Him to help me use them to the fullest, for His glory.

___ Compile a scriptural ABCs (verses beginning with letters of alphabet) to recite during insomnia or waiting times.

✧

48. Writing as Therapy

Read Psalm 61

Hear my cry, O God; attend to my prayer.
Psalm 61:1

An early morning TV program once featured a segment on a camp in Connecticut for seriously ill children. The camp, called "The Hole-in-the-Wall Gang," was founded by actor Paul Newman from profits of his food production business.

The rapt faces of children (with cancer, AIDS, sickle cell anemia, and other maladies) and their bubbly joy in being at camp with one another captured my heart. Yet an aspect of the story that especially intrigued me involved graduate students from a nearby university. They were helping the campers learn to express their deep feelings in writing. Selections read revealed children in tune with themselves, their illness, and the world many would be leaving all too soon.

Reflecting on the incident reminded me of the therapeutic benefits many people find in expressing their innermost feelings on paper. As a biblical example, think of the psalmist David and how he told God of his joys, sorrows, victories, and failures. A seventy-two-year-old friend told me that the anger and anguish that enveloped him following a loved one's suicide sent him to his word processor to pour out his heartache.

Once I acted on an activity suggested by my minister—to write a weekly letter to God during the summer. I soon found the experience enormously liberating, and I looked forward to Saturday morning when I got out my prayer notebook. I continued for several months until I began to keep a daily journal.

Writers report a variety of benefits from the activity:

A safety valve for emotions, as you pour out anger, hurts, frustration, and disappointment to One who always understands.

An aid to decision-making, as you lay out pros and cons of a quandary, interlacing jotting with prayer.

A means of self-discovery, such as a journal-keeper finding "a quiet river within" flowing from his or her deepest being onto paper.

A heightened sense of God's presence, as you list blessings, give thanks for His faithfulness, and seek continuing guidance.

A reinforcement for the future, as you review past trials and joys, noting God's steadfastness.

Whether writing "letters to God," a diary, or just occasional thoughts in a notebook, keep them private. You will write more freely. (You may decide sometime later to share parts.)

✧

My Prayer

Father, thank You for the avenue of writing as one means of talking with You in a personal and private way. Amen.

My Goal

To get closer to God by expressing thoughts on paper.

My Commitment This Week

Choose two or more activities:

___ Write a letter to God, thanking Him for blessings and seeking His guidance for specific situations.

___ Write a letter to God, telling Him about a troubling situation I don't want to discuss with anyone else.

___ Write a letter to a friend, sharing what my faith in God means to me.

___ Buy a notebook and begin a weekly journal, increasing the frequency as desired. Enlist a friend to join me on the writing journey, encouraging one another.

___ Check the library or bookstore for a book on journal writing.

✧

49. Two Birthdays

Read John 3:1–17

Unless one is born again, he cannot see the kingdom of God.
John 3:3

A drawing of a butterfly embellishes the chapter head-
ings of Charles Colson's 1976 best seller *Born Again*. In
an introductory statement he explained: "The butterfly is
nature's most visible illustration of rebirth. Once drab
and earthbound as a caterpillar, the butterfly emerges
from the cocoon in beautifully radiant colors, soaring up-
ward into the sky. Free—BORN AGAIN—just as each
of us can be when we are, through Christ, born again in
the spirit."

Most of us still welcome birthday cards—the ex-
pressions of love from family and friends—even if we've
been receiving them sixty years or more. As we bask in
the brief special attention, our thoughts often slip back-
ward, focusing on images of celebrations past. For
Christians, the day marking our physical birth represents an appropriate time to ponder our spiritual birth
as well. Many people remember the exact occasion
when they asked Christ into their lives. Others don't recall the specifics but know they belong to Him and
sense His Spirit within. Some find the idea of a second
birth confusing.

Nicodemus, a respected Jewish leader to whom Jesus
explained the need to be "born again," also found the notion confusing. Nicodemus recognized Christ as being
sent from God because of the miraculous things He was
doing. So he went to Him at night to find out more.
When told that to enter the kingdom of God one must
be born again, Nicodemus asked if he had to revert to
embryonic form and re-enter his mother's womb.

Jesus told His questioner not to confuse the flesh with the Spirit. Then He likened the Spirit to the wind: you hear the sound of it, but you can't see where it comes from or where it goes. In effect, He was telling this learned teacher that the power of the Spirit cannot be fully understood. By accepting God's Son as Savior and being obedient to the Holy Spirit's leading, however one will experience the new birth.

As part of Jesus' discourse on the new birth, He reminded us *why* and *how* it came about: "For God so loved the world that He gave His only begotten Son, that whoever believes in Him should not perish but have everlasting life" (John 3:16).

✧

My Prayer

Father, thank You for the new birth that assures me of eternal life. Guide my meditations this week, that I may seek not so much to understand as to yield my life afresh to Your guidance, so that Your radiance will be reflected for all to see. Amen.

My Goal

To yield my life afresh to God's complete control.

My Commitment This Week

Choose two or more activities:

___ Thank God for giving His son and for inviting me to accept Him as Lord so that I am assured of eternal life.

___ Each morning, ask God to fill my total being with His Holy Spirit—to direct my thoughts, words, and actions—so my life honors Him.

___ Pray the hymn "Spirit of God, Descend upon My Heart."

___ Ask respected Christian friends to comment on their understanding of the new birth.

___ Read *The Holy Spirit* by Billy Graham (or another book about the Third Person of the Trinity).

50. God's Answer to Worry

Read Philippians 4:4–9

Don't worry over anything whatever; tell God every detail of your needs in earnest and thankful prayer.
Philippians 4:6, PHILLIPS

A cloud of guilt envelops me when I begin drifting into worry. I'm grateful for the guilt because it gently reminds me of the powerful lesson my mother (at sixty-eight) taught me about the subject.

Mother had flown to Houston to join her sister, who was undergoing treatment for cancer at M. D. Anderson Hospital. My aunt's negative prognosis prompted my decision to join them for a few days. My flight from Chicago was due in Houston about 9:00 P.M.

Equipment problems developed in the connecting plane out of St. Louis, and we wound up on a runway in a small town in Arkansas. We received periodic apologies and revised estimates about departures as we waited several hours. Airline personnel assured us that information about our flight had been relayed to Houston and would be passed along to anyone inquiring. We finally landed there at 7:00 A.M.

A call from the airport produced the incredible news that my mother knew nothing of our all-night problems. "They insisted your plane arrived on time and that you must have missed it," she said. Yet when I got to her room she looked rested and relaxed.

"I see you didn't lose any sleep worrying," I said.

"Oh, I had a good night's rest," she said. "After checking the airport, I called Chicago, and Helen said you made the plane. She had also talked to folks in St. Louis who said you made the connecting flight."

"But I wasn't here," I protested, puzzled.

"I'd done all I could," she said. "So I prayed and simply turned it over to God. I knew if you were all right I may as well get my sleep. And if something had happened to you, I'd need all my strength to stand it." Then she added, "Don't you think I did the right thing?"

"Brilliant response," I said, laughing. I've tried to follow her example when worries threaten to destroy my peace and steal sleep. These steps work for me:

✧ *Pray about possible actions* to take to help resolve the problem. Sometimes I pray with a Christian friend.

✧ *Claim God's promise* to accept the burden and thank Him for what He will do. Ask Him to stop me from "taking the problem back."

✧ *Focus thoughts and energy* on more productive pursuits. My continuous to do list provides fruitful ideas.

Invariably, I experience God's mysterious peace—the kind that permitted my mother a refreshing night's sleep—even when I have no clue about the problem's solution.

✧

My Prayer

Father, help me to remember the futility of worry and to release anxieties to You in gratitude. Amen.

My Goal

To learn to trust God to handle my worries.

My Commitment This Week

Choose two or more activities:

___ Ask the Lord to help me understand the futility of worry and to learn to leave my problems with Him.

___ Think about difficult situations the Lord has helped me through in the past and give thanks.

___ Apply the steps in this meditation to any problems.

___ Memorize Philippians 4:6–7. Share it with a worrier.

___ Pray about whether there is anything tangible I can do to help someone who is facing a major problem.

51. The Role Model

Read Luke 18:31–43

He steadfastly set His face to go to Jerusalem.
Luke 9:51

In the classic best-seller *In His Steps* (first published in 1897), Charles M. Sheldon tells the story of a young minister in Topeka, Kansas, who issues an astounding proposition to his congregation. He asks volunteers to pledge themselves earnestly and honestly for a year not to do anything without first asking, "What would Jesus do?" The experiment changes the lives of an entire town.

George, beset by severe health problems in his late eighties, inspired many of us by his cheerful disposition, his interest in others, and his desire to continue learning (though he held several degrees). His upbeat approach to life resulted from his scrutiny of the life of Jesus.

"Jesus' actions," he said, "as He knowingly approached His agonizing betrayal and death, provide the ultimate role model for Christians, especially when beset with mental or physical pain."

Reviewing highlights of Jesus' journey as He completed His Father's assignments provides evidence of the supernatural guidance and strength available to His followers. In Galilee, Jesus reminded His disciples He would be killed. As He continued toward Jerusalem, He also continued training the twelve He had called.

A little child was held up by Jesus to help His disciples understand the need for humility and the dire consequences of causing a believer to stumble. He used parables to emphasize desirable character traits, such as the need to forgive, and the faithful use of one's talents. He counseled the rich young ruler about how to inherit eternal life. When Zacchaeus climbed a sycamore tree for a better view of Jesus, He visited his home, resulting in salvation for the household.

Jesus restored the sight of the blind beggar Bartimaeus when He was near Jericho. Passing through a village, He paused to heal ten lepers. As He approached Jerusalem, He wept over the city. At the temple, He became angry at those desecrating it by buying and selling, and began to drive them out. He continued teaching there daily even though the chief priests, scribes, and leaders were seeking to destroy Him.

The bottom line for George: "Although weighed down by terrible grief, Jesus continued resolutely with His mission. Can we do likewise?"

✧

My Prayer

*Father, thank You for the role model You provided
in Your Son. Guide me in pursuing Your will
for me. Amen.*

My Goal

To try to follow the example of Jesus and accomplish God's will for my life.

My Commitment This Week

Choose two or more activities:

___ Pray that I will learn to know Jesus better and follow Him more closely.

___ When in doubt about a course of action, ask myself, "What would Jesus do?"

___ Write down and meditate on who Jesus says He is in these passages: John 6:35; 8:12; 10:7; 10:11; 11:25.

___ Read Luke 22:24–30 for a reminder of Jesus' example about service to others.

___ Read *In His Steps* by Charles M. Sheldon or the updated version, *What Would Jesus Do?* by his great-grandson, Garrett Sheldon.

52. Manna for Today

Read John 6:22–40

He humbled you, causing you to hunger and then feeding you with manna . . . to teach you that man does not live on bread alone but on every word that comes from the mouth of the Lord.
Deuteronomy 8:3, NIV

Bread making, which I took up soon after retirement, ranks as one of my most satisfying activities. A gift of sour dough starter launched the venture and set the schedule, since it requires weekly depletion and "feeding." Great joy pervades both the process, especially kneading, and the sharing of the results.

Perhaps my devotion to making bread fueled my excitement in learning the spiritual truths about manna, when studying the life of Moses. Manna appeared as a gift of God to feed the Israelites during their years of wilderness wanderings. The small white substance fell to the ground each morning except the Sabbath.

Deuteronomy 8:3 states that the purpose of manna: is to remind people that they should not live by bread alone but by the Word of God. Jesus quoted from the verse when Satan tempted Him to turn stones into bread.

The day after Jesus fed the five thousand, people asked Jesus for a sign so that they could believe in Him, reminding Him of the manna that sustained their forefathers in the desert. Jesus said God had provided the bread from heaven. Then he told them that He Himself was the true bread sent down by His Father. "I am the bread of life" (John 6:35), He declared.

The manna of the Old Testament thus stands as a symbol for Christ. Examining the parallels reinforces the importance of feeding on the Word of God, to be empowered by the Son.

Bible study calls for a regular schedule. The Israelites received manna as a free gift, just as we receive Scripture; but they were required to gather a fresh supply each morning. We benefit most if we get into the Word on a regular basis.

Bible study demands diligence. After it was gathered, manna had to be ground with a handmill or crushed in a mortar, and then cooked, making cakes of it. Similarly, if we're to digest Scripture, we must concentrate on it, carefully searching out its meaning and application under the Holy Spirit's guidance.

The need for Bible study remains for a lifetime. The manna provided physical nourishment for the people during the entire forty years they roamed the wilderness. The Word of God provides spiritual nourishment throughout our earthly pilgrimage. That spiritual food arrives new every morning, as did the manna.

Diligent Bible study helps us know Christ, the Bread of life, and follow His teaching, insuring a fulfilled life.

✧

My Prayer

Father, give me the discipline to get into Your Word in an organized way so that I can become a better disciple. Amen.

My Goal

To become a more effective student of the Bible.

My Commitment This Week

___ Choose two or more activities:

___ Thank God for the Bible and for His Holy Spirit to help me understand it and apply it to my life.

___ Ask God to help me think through my Bible study habits and make changes needed to strengthen them.

___ Pray about organizing a home Bible study group with rotating leadership. (A Christian bookstore has good group study guides.)

___ Challenge a friend to study the focus passage of this meditation (John 6:22–40). Meet for coffee and discussion.

___ Take a gift of bread to a friend.

Source Notes

Week 1.

Gwen Lam, "Wakc-Up Call," *Decision* (January 1984).

Week 2.

Linda A. Charles, "Carver Legacy Remembered," *The Iowa Stater* (February 1991).

Week 4.

Frank Wilcox, "I Believe in the Communion of Saints," *The Good Samaritan* (Fall 1994). Used by permission.

Week 7

Amy Carmichael, *Edges of His Ways* (Fort Washington, Penn.: Christian Literature Crusade, 1975), 137.

Week 9

Catherine Marshall, *A Closer Walk* (Old Tappan, N. J.: Chosen Books, Fleming H. Revell Company, 1986), 99–100.

Week 11

Corrie ten Boom, *Clippings from My Notebook* (Nashville: Thomas Nelson Publishers, 1982), 92–94. Reprinted from *Guideposts* (1972).

Week 14

Gwen Lam, "Sunday Morning Worship Menu," *Christian Single* (September 1983).

Week 15

Hannah Whitall Smith, *The God of All Comfort* (Chicago: Moody Press, 1956), 7.

Week 19

Sarah and A. Elizabeth Delany with Amy Hill Hearth, *The Delany Sisters' Book of Everyday Wisdom* (New York: Kodansha America, Inc., 1994), 4, 44–45.

Week 21

Ray Lam with Gwen Lam, "Left Hand Miracle," *Independent Living & Health Care Today* (Fall 1988).

Week 22

"Norman Cousins Helps Other Patients as He Once Helped Himself—by Laughing," *Good Housekeeping* (November 1989). Adapted from Norman Cousins, *Head First: the Biology of Hope* (New York: E. P. Dutton, 1989).

Week 23

Archibald Rutledge, *Life's Extras* (Westwood, N. J.: Fleming H. Revell Company, 1978), 5, 14–16.

Week 30.

C. S. Lewis, *Surprised by Joy* (New York: Harcourt, Brace, & World, Inc., 1955), VII.

Week 31

Paul Tournier, *The Adventure of Living* (New York: Harper & Row, 1976), 9.

Week 32

Phillip Keller, *A Shepherd Looks at Psalm 23* (Grand Rapids, Mich.: Zondervan Publishing House, 1977), 20–21, 36, 42, 52.

Week 35

Richard Corliss, "The Last Leading Lady," *Time* (September 26, 1994).

Week 49

Charles W. Colson, *Born Again* (Old Tappan, N. J.: Chosen Books, 1976), Introductory Statement.

Week 51

Charles M. Sheldon, *In His Steps* (Nashville, Tenn.: Broadman & Holman Publishers, 1995).